GIRLS ARE OUR FUTURE

"This is not a biography but rather a compilation of Sister Cyril's thoughts on a number of topics: education, life, sexuality, social life, and religion, interspersed with jokes, interviews with staff and students, and comments from alums. At the end of this romp through a life of giving and doing and developing programs to embrace more children and adults in opportunities to improve their lives, one agrees with Sister Cyril that 'Life is energy. Life is joy. Life is happiness. Life is living. Life is movement.'

In this chaotic world, Sister Cyril's words are like a soothing balm. She doesn't give us the answers — although she has some very smart ideas and guidelines — but 'talks' to us employing humor, common sense, anecdotes, and examples of successes and some failures. Her perspective is refreshing and inspires one to look around, see the good in people, assess where there is need, and then, GET BUSY."

—Geraldine Forbes, Distinguished Professor Emerita, State University of New York Oswego

"This book allowed me to delve into my own practice, to question, compare and to take insights that profoundly affected my dealings with my own students. It was also through reading and hearing Sister Cyril's stories that gave rise to my need to help empower young people, especially the underprivileged children in my back yard. It reminded me of 'Tuesdays with Morrie'—each page giving you more insight on how to be a better person and help the world we live in. A truly inspiring read."

—Catherine Rankin, Drama Teacher, Manila

"As an educator, I constantly question the purpose of my job, as a woman I often wonder if my voice is being heard, as a parent of two young women I fear for the future of the world. Reading this book has given me hope. It is a story of a woman, or rather a force, who sees education as liberation. She has made it her job to empower so many young women, many of whom may not otherwise have had a chance in this world. It is a book about faith but it does not preach faith. It suggests that having an individual faith is crucial to getting the job done. It is not a book about how to make friends and influence people, but it will influence people. I offered some passages to my young trainee teachers as a starting point for a discussion about the purpose of education. They suggested that even after twelve years in school and three years of studying education in university, they could never come up with an answer. Having read about Sister Cyril's Rainbow Children, they now know the answer."

—Becky Patterson, Manchester Metropolitan University, Faculty of Education

"Sister Cyril is a phenomenon. In her own words a 'practical radical' blessed with extraordinary energy and determination, and an incredibly optimistic outlook on the world. So what is it like to spend time in the company of such a person? I did just that on a number of annual visits to Loreto School where I helped out in a minor organisational capacity—and I have never been the same since. Now it is possible for people not fortunate enough to have had such first hand experience to get to know her through this book. Her authentic voice comes straight off the page with all the intelligence, humour, wisdom, idiosyncrasy and often sheer stubbornness that characterise the woman. And above all, you feel her love and understanding that have influenced the lives of so many people lucky enough to have known her. Be prepared to be challenged and inspired by what you read here. If you open your heart to Sister Cyril's words, I promise you too will be changed by them."

—Rachel Douglas, friend of Sister Cyril

"You never stop learning. I think I have learnt more about being human from Sister Cyril's stories, her interviews, and the musings contained within these pages than I have from a lifetime of studying our western quest for happiness.

This is a book that needs to be read slowly, contemplatively and again. So much of life is covered. I imagine the content will ruffle some feathers. I am sure that some readers will be shocked at the forthrightness of Sister Cyril's viewpoints, her (refreshing) disregard for political correctness. Who cares? Not Sister Cyril, of that I'm sure. There are lessons here for teachers, parents, doctors, makers of policies and guardians of purse strings. As I reluctantly came to the last page I reflected on who else I would like to read this book. My list was long and rich. The world needs practical radicalism and it needs it now."

—Mike Scanlan, Consultant Nurse in Mental Health and Wellbeing

GIRLS ARE OUR FUTURE

Thoughts of a Practical, Radical Nun

By

Sister Cyril

and

Neil Farrelly

&

Greg Dale

Konark Publishers Pvt Ltd
New Delhi · Seattle

Konark Publishers Pvt. Ltd
206, First Floor,
Peacock Lane, Shahpur Jat,
New Delhi-110 049.
Phone: +91-11-41055065, 65254972
e-mail: india@konarkpublishers.com
Website: www.konarkpublishers.com

Konark Publishers International
8615, 13th Ave SW,
Seattle, WA 98106
Phone: (415) 409-9988
e-mail: us@konarkpublishers.com

Cataloging in Publication Data--DK

Courtesy: D.K. Agencies (P) Ltd. <docinfo@dkagencies.com>

Cyril, *Sister*, **author**.

Girls are our future : thoughts of a practical, radical nun/by Sister Cyril and Neil Farrelly & Greg Dale.

pages cm

ISBN 9789322008833

1. Thought and thinking. 2. Cyril, Sister. I. Farrelly, Neil, author. II. Dale, Gregory A., author. III. Title.

BF441.C97 2017 DDC 153.42 23

Editor: Teesta Guha Sarkar

Illustrations by Minori Kawakami

Photos by Dominic Mann and Gianluigi Nocco

Typeset by Saanvi Graphics, Noida

Printed and bound at Thomson Press (India) Ltd.

Our aim...
is not to show the world the state of the Present—
it is to show the world what we can make of the Future.

—Loreto Alumni

Some people come into our lives and quickly go. Some stay a while, leave footprints in our hearts, and we are never, ever the same.

—Loreto Teacher

Contents

PREFACE

BY NEIL FARRELLY

In 2007, we were in Kolkata and were told Sister Cyril could give us ten minutes for an interview. Ten minutes became thirty, when she suddenly said, "I like your questions. I'm 72 years old, and I want to write a book about all of this before I die. Can you do it?"

I asked her what kind of book she wanted it to be. "My God, certainly not one of those holier-than-thou books!" What she didn't want was to write her autobiography. So, after starting in 2009, we returned many times to interview her and talk with her students, teachers and friends, to put together the story of her life. This is that book.

Sister Cyril is a force. Creative, both spiritual and practical in the same breath, she has strong bones and couldn't remember when she last got sick (she lives in, quite possibly, one of the most polluted places on earth), she is fearless, controversial, sometimes irritable, at times overbearing, has been awarded numerous accolades and honorary doctorates, wears a nun's habit together with sturdy black boots, possesses a photographic memory, a conscience that never quits, and enough stamina to fuel the city of Kolkata all by herself.

She's not a saint but that's not what she cares about.

She reminded me of Hotei, a laughing Buddha, who used to teach enlightenment by walking into town and laughing. His laughter was so infectious that everyone in the village began laughing, too, and when people asked him for enlightenment, he would laugh until he cried.

I know for a fact that she does not need us all to agree with her about what she says here, but what she does fervently want is for people to stop and think.

You may find some of her words hard, tough, some of her remedies unorthodox, but that has a lot to do with the context in which these problems are happening, an everyday reality that would smother most of us. It's difficult to imagine that kind of existence, and how strong you have to be to live inside it.

God. Religion. Jesus Christ. Catholicism. Priests. She is only too aware of people's fears and prejudices when they hear these words, and I think she's trying to get beyond all of that. God is not in any book she knows, or is anything she can easily describe in words. What religion you follow matters not one iota—she's lived with a billion Hindus and Muslims for the past 50 years. Whether you believe in her God or any other is immaterial to her and her peace of mind. You go your way, she'll go her way, and she'll see you in heaven one day.

PART I

Opening Thoughts

Imagine This…

This Place, Kolkata

This Place, Loreto

How Do Girls Get into Loreto?

Rescuing a Child

Who Are the Rainbow Children and How Did It All Start?

Conversation on an Overpass (interview)

IMAGINE THIS...

I have one pair of shoes.

I have two or three others, but only one pair that I wear. I wear only one pair of shoes at a time. It's all we can do; we've only got two feet. Until the shoes die; then I wear another pair.

I have a vow of poverty.

I don't own anything, as such, so I don't have anything to give up either.

Theoretically, if my superiors asked me for my car tomorrow, I'd give it to them.

So what do I have?

I have the clothes I'm wearing, and some others. A pen. A mobile phone. Spectacles, some books, my thesis, lots of paper.

Of course, I have this whole school, more or less, but I can't claim any of it. In theory I have it, but at any time, I might have to give it up.

The school cats are very precious to me, especially the little black-and-white one, but even the cats are not possessions because they can walk off whenever they want.

We don't own them.

What else? What else?

A bed to sleep on, a towel to wipe my face, soap, a comb for my hair. I can't think of anything else. Put like this, it seems so silly, puerile, doesn't it?

I have all kinds of little knick-knacks that people have given me, but I don't see them as my possessions because they're lying around all over the place, and I wish people wouldn't give them to me. At the same time, I'm grateful for their kind thought, and so I keep them out of respect for their feelings.

What's the use of any of that stuff? That's my question: what use is it?

But I keep this pretty shell because I like to tell people about the sea, the seagull, the wind and the shell.

Once upon a time, the sea thought she would like to share her sweet song with everyone. So she decided to have a training session, which the seagull, the wind and the shell all agreed to attend. They started well, but at the coffee break, the seagull remembered some pressing engagement and flew off, by the afternoon the wind had completely lost interest and went to blow somewhere else, which left only the shell, who stayed till the very end. And that is why, even now, the seagull has only its harsh cry, the wind has only its mournful whistle, while, if you hold the shell up to your ear, you can hear the sweet music of the sea.

THIS PLACE, KOLKATA

A metropolitan sprawl of about 15 million, packed into 728 square miles. People everywhere, dashing for trams and buses, which stop anywhere and hold up all the traffic. Two hundred thousand people pass by the school gates every morning and every evening. If you stand on the footbridge across the road outside the school and look down, you would think you were looking at two rivers, which are in fact human heads flowing up the street towards the station and down the street away from it.

If you want to visualize how many people we have in Kolkata, put them across the road outside the gate, ten abreast and march them past day and night, and even after two whole years you will not have seen the last of them! So it is not difficult to believe the story about the man who refused to pay his fare on the bus because he claimed he was never actually on the bus. He was simply holding on to someone, who was holding on to someone, who was holding on to someone, who was holding on to the bus! He never touched the bus, so why should he pay?

There are things that happen in Kolkata which would drive people in the West mad. For example, I sat for hours in solid traffic yesterday, because the police had blocked off all the roads for a big political rally they held in the narrowest part of the main street!

For me, this personifies Kolkata and the general chaos of the place. It's nice because you never have to be on time for anything; you can always blame it on the traffic jams, claim that the website was down, or the telephone didn't work, that there was no water, or a power cut caused delays; there are lots of excuses for not doing your job.

But, the city works! I know we have power cuts, yes, but we've got two generators at the school. We had to buy them recently, in desperation, because our computers wouldn't work, and once they were off, what could we do? We manage, and you do get used to it all because your expectations are nil. So you wake up and are grateful the fans are running and it's cool, and if nothing is working, well, you didn't expect it to anyway.

That's the way we live here. There's a resilience and a capacity to take hardship without too much grumbling. There's a whole different way of seeing life, accepting things.

People in the West have much higher expectations.

Look at New Orleans and Hurricane Katrina, when the river overflowed and the city was inundated and thousands of people were displaced and put into halls, gyms, and listen to the racket they all made about it! Here in South Asia, we had the tsunami around the same time, where millions and millions of people were displaced, and you barely heard a murmur; they just all picked themselves up and went on with life.

In Chennai, one of our sisters was standing by the beach when she saw this great big, black cloud coming in from the sea. People around her were selling things, eating, drinking tea, and she said it came in so fast she only had time to grab hold of an iron railing and wrap herself around it. The tsunami washed over her and tore off half of her clothes. After it had passed, she opened her eyes and found all the cars had gone, all the beach sellers had been washed away, and the church crypt, from where she had just come after Mass, was full of water drowning both her uncle and aunt.

She always cries when she talks about it.

THIS PLACE, LORETO

People's first impression of this place is exactly the same as Kolkata: Chaos.

But if they lingered a little longer, they'd see that under the chaos is a great deal of order, that everybody is doing their own thing and everybody knows what it is they are supposed to be doing, and that life is going along quite smoothly, and people might become intrigued enough about the place to start asking questions, and we would try and answer them, and that would lead them farther into this jungle, and somewhere in the middle of it all they might find me.

But you need to take the time to see that, and if you arrive here with any preconceived notions, we can't do anything to help you. You'll need an open mind.

Here's an example:

People come in wanting to start a new programme for the poor—they're looking for new ideas—so I say, "Would you like to look around the place, see the Rainbow children?" And they all say "Oh yes!" and up they go, and when they come back down they have two different reactions.

The first type comes back in five minutes, and tells me, "You know, Sister, I'm very busy, I have a lot of work to do while I'm in Kolkata, so excuse me now, I'm off," and we say goodbye. Fine.

The other type comes down thirty minutes later, very excited, and says, "Hey, you've got so much stuff going on up there; could I copy some of this? I can see this would be very useful for my tribal children up in the Northeast."

They're both seeing the same thing, they're both here ostensibly to help the poor, but the first one will never get anywhere, because he only sees the poor in an idealized way. Whereas the second one is practical and has enough imagination that when he sees something unique, he is immediately caught by it. No one, though, walks away untouched. Well, no women walk away untouched. Some men do. Mostly priests.

Women see possibilities. Men are more fixed in what they're already doing themselves, and they can be hard to move. Men are different from women, no doubt about it, and when people say we're all alike, well? Our psychologies are very different. When females get together, they talk about people, about each other. Men talk about sports, the scores, the latest BMW's. Of course, I'm generally not a companion when men talk amongst themselves but that's my impression.

I do a test with mixed groups by giving them a long list of stuff and telling them to, as quickly as possible, tick all the things they like on that list; the boys tick things, whereas the girls tick people.

HOW DO GIRLS GET INTO LORETO?

Girls get into Loreto by lottery. In an education system which promotes competition in even the 'best' schools, admission tests are designed to cream off the best little brains, and parents begin grooming their offspring from the time they are two years old or even younger! With tutors and coaching classes, all very expensive, where does the poor child stand?

We take 50 percent from the well-off sector and 50 percent from the poorest. For admission to the Rainbow programme, need is the criterion, and we take in as many as we can.

The parents of the well-off children pay the full fee, which goes to teachers' salaries since the government doesn't help. They are aware of the number of poor children the school supports and frequently donate uniforms and other clothes, shoes and books in good condition for recycling. Once, a House Captain came to me with three sets of new uniforms and asked me to give them to a certain girl in her House. She explained that she had seen this girl wearing a cardigan that wasn't part of the uniform and had insisted that she remove it. The girl was reluctant and when the Captain saw the condition of her uniform under the cardigan—mended in many places and so worn down that there was almost no cloth left—she felt so ashamed that she had so much and this girl had next to nothing, that she went home and asked her mother if they could buy some uniforms for her. But she did not wish to embarrass her by giving them to her directly, and asked me to hand them over instead.

Who says inclusion cannot work?

Slum-dwelling children who cannot afford to pay tuition fees and need full financial support come in at four years of age along with those who pay. They get their uniforms and books for free from the school as well as food (a hot midday meal) and even rations to take home as they are so badly off. They get an evening snack before they go home, and very often you will see them slipping it carefully into their bags to take back to their mothers who may have had nothing to eat all day. If they have younger siblings, the children are encouraged to take a meal home to them as well so they are not brain-damaged when it is their turn to go to school. They live in hutments stitched together from bits of sacking, rags, cardboard, and it is a source of wonder how they come here so clean. They have the option to stay and study in school, if they have no place at home. They can also even have a bath here, especially when they grow older and are bigger. We do everything we can to ensure that they get a fair chance and take pride in their progress.

Rainbow children also need full support, sometimes as day scholars but more often for living in the Rainbow Home. Those who come off the street very young are incorporated straightaway into the Nursery grade of the English-medium school where they pick up English very fast. If they come off the street at ten or eleven they are prepared for Bengali medium so they are not held back by their lack of English, which they pick up as they move up in school. Interaction with the English-medium children facilitates this.

Living on the street has, in many cases, robbed these children of their entire primary schooling, so it is important that they catch up at an accelerated rate and emerge in Class 12 at par with their more privileged peer group.

RESCUING A CHILD

It was a holiday and he came through the gate around 9:00 in the morning. He had a baby in his arms and two little toddlers trailing behind. He took them over to the tap, took off the rags they had on and proceeded to bathe them. Then out of the little plastic bag he carried, he took three little clean dresses and clothed them.

He was their brother, all of seven years old!

They spent the day in school, observing all the activities and taking part in some. The older students said to me, "The baby needs milk," so I said, "What will we do?"

"We can buy milk from the shop and a baby's feeding bottle."

"OK," I said. "Do that." So the baby was fed and the others, too, and when evening came we found an old cot that someone had donated, cleaned it up and put in a fresh mattress and bedding for the baby, and the other three just curled up on a big mat like little puppies and fell asleep.

It was a very wet night and their mother came in around 10 pm looking for them. She explained that she had to work at a mango stall and couldn't leave it, and her son had taken the children and wandered off, and when she came searching, the people on the street told her they were safe in the school. It was raining heavily so I asked her where she would spend the night. She said, "Oh, under the bridge or in some shop doorway."

"Would you like to leave them here?"

Her face lit up. “Oh, yes,” she said, and so they stayed.

It doesn’t take much to rescue a child if you keep your gate and your heart open! We sent the boy over to the Salesians, who have a wonderful set-up for boys from the street, but he was so worried about his mother that he kept running away to go back to her. Likewise for the sister immediately after him, but the other two and several siblings born later are still with us. The youngest is now in Class 4 in our English-medium school, a good example of how important it is to bring children in as early as possible, while also allowing them to be free.

Children from the streets are free spirits. That’s why we call them Rainbows.

A rainbow gives us great joy when we see it in the sky, but we can’t pin down a rainbow. We can only commune with it.

WHO ARE THE RAINBOW CHILDREN AND HOW DID IT ALL START?

Way back in 1979, when I joined Loreto Sealdah as Principal, I attempted to carry out a survey of street children, and so with great éclat, I showed the teachers and students how to conduct interviews and I sent them all out, and they came back and said, "No, there's nobody poor on the street; the children are all quite fat." Neither teachers nor students were able to recognize the deprivation before them—malnourishment causing people's stomachs to swell up—as they had never been compelled to actually observe these realities.

So my next move was to send them all out to the rural areas, and soon they were able to "see" the poor people, and after a few years, they asked me, "Can't we bring them in?" "Go ahead," I told them. "It can be your project. I'm too busy now, so you bring them in but do not promise anything and do nothing to rid them of their survival skills."

So they went out on their own and brought the street children back in here, and that's when the Rainbow programme began. The children started coming in after school, and as time went by they came earlier and earlier, and I realized that we could easily accommodate them throughout the day and let the regular kids teach them during their work education classes.

At first we only got boys, and they were so wild we had our neatly uniformed girls racing around the school compound trying to grab them and make them sit down to study! Then we had the little fellow who was reported for having taken six eggs on his plate at lunchtime. I went over to him and he had three eggs on his plate and three more stuffed in his scarf around his waist. I picked him up by the collar, took away his plate and the other eggs from around his waist and told him, "In school, you get one egg for one boy, so out you go and come back when you get manners," and I put him out the gate. Next morning he was back in, grinning away, "Namashkar, Sister!" and no more trouble. And no more extra eggs taken either!

Finally, we asked the street girls why none of them came in, and they told us, "We get harassed enough on the streets by the boys; why should we come in here for more?" So eventually, we got another NGO to take the boys, and we filled up with girls who were very glad to come on their own. However, we still send our students over to help teach the boys.

Then one night, a three-year-old girl, living on the street with her parents, was raped, and I realized how vulnerable girls were at night, even with parents, and more so without them. I looked around and saw our school lying empty every evening from 4:00 when the students go home to 8:00 the next morning when they return, and all that lovely space wasted.

Could we not use it to provide a safe place for the girls to sleep and live in?

And so the first Rainbow Home was born with twenty girls, and a couple of boys whom we sent off to the Brothers as early as possible.

Since then, enrollment has risen to 240, and there are always so many people looking to get their children in that we have had to put a strict background check policy in place to ensure that there is room for the most needy. One old grandmother was making a case in favour of our taking her little girl into the Home, weeping copiously, claiming the parents were dead. Our social worker called the little one aside and asked her what colour shirt her father was wearing that morning. She replied that he was wearing a green shirt and her mommy was in a blue sari. Human nature being what it is, there are as many people in India ready to avail themselves of free handouts as in the rest of the world! And more power to them if they fool us because we haven't done our homework!

Now the concept has spread to other Loreto schools, so we have maybe 700 girls off the streets in our schools alone, and then there are also Homes in Delhi, Hyderabad, Chennai, Bengaluru and other places.

CONVERSATION ON AN OVERPASS

This interview was conducted on a busy footbridge spanning a crowded road that runs right past the front gates of Loreto, in the heart of Kolkata.

What's your favourite book?

Oh, I have millions of favourite books, I can't tell you that. What can I say? I have so many!

What about food?

Chinese. I love Chinese, ordinary chow mein. I wouldn't even know the names of all the others things I like.

What's the meaning of life?

The meaning of life? You're asking me that on a road like this, with such a crowd around us? This is life, isn't it? In the middle of Kolkata, this city is pulsating with life. Life is energy. Life is joy. Life is happiness. Life is living. Life is movement. How many times can I say what life is?

In case you're interested, right over there is the NRS Hospital. It handles 30,000 outpatients every day. You have to get in there by 9:00 am, take a ticket, and wait for your turn.

I went to get a sore in my mouth seen to, and they took me into a big room full of people, with three doctors sitting at a table. One of them told me to open my mouth, so I did, and he looked in. But then all the other patients in the room crowded around, wanting to have a look in as well! And everyone offered an opinion on what they saw, because everyone in this city has an opinion on everything, so I'm surprised we haven't had lots of people butting into our conversation.

Do we make our own reality?

I think to some extent we do. Basically, we inherit a reality—there is always one around us—and we interact with that reality to build our own.

Have you ever given up?

No, definitely not! I have never given up and I have no intention of giving up either! I am one of those tenacious types, always trying something new, something better.

Are poor people really poor and rich people really rich?

Yes, poor people are really poor, so poor that they have no voice, and in many cases, no food. Rich people are not really rich. They're only rich by comparison.

In my school, the children who pay fees, it would be the very rare one who had a car, and one in a million who had two. Everything here is priced the same as in England. If I want to buy an oven or a washing machine, they're exactly the same price. But the salaries here are only about one-tenth of your salaries, so that makes even the rich people poor by comparison. But even they are rich compared to the really terrible poverty here.

In Britain, if you are a teacher, for example, you could afford to come to India for a holiday or work here almost every year if you wanted to, whereas, for Indians, it would be a lifetime effort to leave even once.

The salaries are going up, it's better now, but the parents are having a hard time trying to find the money to pay the fees for their children.

Initially, I had 700 paying parents, but now that the fees have gone up, I've only got 500 parents who can afford it. Others pay part of the fee, and the rest pay virtually nothing. That's how it is.

So, does love conquer all?

Does love conquer all? I think in the long run it probably does, it certainly conquers more than anything else does, but I'm not sure if it conquers everything. Hate doesn't conquer anything at all. At least, love reaches into people's hearts, but not all people's hearts are changed by love. Sometimes it takes a little longer than others.

Is everything for a reason, or is it all just chance?

I think everything is for a reason. Ultimately, yes. Because God is behind it all and once God is there, everything holds together. It's sane. But it doesn't mean that everything is perfect. Does that answer your question?

When was the last time you despaired about anything?

Never. I've never despaired about anything. Never, never, never. Despair is not a part of my vocabulary. Two things are not in my character: despair is one, guilt is the other. I'm very fortunate I never feel guilty. Guilt for me is a very negative emotion, and it doesn't get you anywhere. You spend all your time looking back at all the things you've done wrong and feeling sorry for yourself.

So, good comes out of bad?

First, we have to question what is bad. Good and bad are two sides of the same coin. In Hinduism there is no bad. It's all relative...

Oh my, look at the man crossing the road, can you believe it?

It's a fine line between life and death here, but life is very strong. Survival. When you see it like this in front of you, an old man trying to cross the road and that car just misses him like that.

Sometime back, two mothers and their sons went across this road, came out from behind a truck, and were knocked down flat. And the tragedy was that one mother was killed and her little boy survived, and the other mother survived, but her boy died.

And some other parents ran into the office and said, "Sister, Sister, come out to the road and pray for them now!" The one thing they wanted from me was a prayer, that's all they wanted from me, so I went out and prayed over them. I remember about six doctors working over them, one of the mothers dead with a sheet over her, and her boy saying, "Is my mummy going to be alright?" And I told him that "your mummy is away just now, so close your eyes and sleep awhile." Poor little scrap. The other boy was dead on the street, but his mother was alive downstairs. So sad, so sad.

And this bridge was put up especially for our Loreto School to make sure all of us get safely across the road, but do you think any of our children use it? Not on your life! They just take their life into their hands and run across...

Do you have any more questions?

What's your favorite word?

Love. L-O-V-E.

INTERLUDE

A SIKH JOKE...

This is a story about a Sikh who ran the whole way home behind the bus—in Ireland, we have Kerry-man jokes—in India we have Sikh jokes. So, he ran the whole way behind the bus, and he came into his house panting, looking like he was going to have a heart attack.

His wife ran to get him a cup of coffee.

"You know," he said, wheezing, "I ran the whole way behind the bus today and saved 1 rupee!"

She looked at him and said, "Oh, you old fool, why didn't you run all the way home behind a taxi and save 50 rupees?!"

A FEW WORDS FROM A STUDENT

I've been at Loreto from 2004. I've learned many things: how to manage the younger children, how we have to understand their feelings, as to what they want and what they want from us.

I have a mother and grandmother. My father died when I was 11 years old, so we are very poor, very poor.

When I say I'm poor, I mean, I don't have my own house; it's not big, we have to pay for rent. My mother works in a nursing home, she's not a nurse but she helps the patients. My mother cooks for all of us. We have a bed for me, my mother, my grandmother and my sister.

It's not such a bad background, but, by my age, 17, many, many girls have got married. If I lived at home, not here, I would also have to get married because we're so poor. Indian culture is very different to other cultures. When girls are growing up here, their mothers think about them, worry about them, and are afraid for them a lot.

When I'm at home, I can't study because of the environment. There are many bad people around my house, and so if I get married we will be able to support my parents and the boy's parents. But now, I think I can manage by myself, so I'm here, at Loreto.

My family still thinks I have to marry, it's a fact. They think I'm still very small so when I'm going from Loreto back to my home I must not go alone, they must come and get me. Though I don't think my mother worries about me as much as she did.

Soon I'll be 18. When I was young, I felt shy to talk to other persons. Now, I'm not shy because I became smart. I've had all kinds of changes in my life. I've grown a lot since last year.

My country is a very poor country and many children don't have a chance to study, so I think in the future, I'll help them, and if they study, they'll also be changed like me, and they'll do something for their families. Because we come from very poor families, we can improve and get nice jobs.

Our families are doing a lot for us right now, so we can do something for them in the future.

I want to be a lawyer, a criminal lawyer. Or a businesswoman.

...AND A TEACHER

I'm an ex-student of this school, I studied here and Sister Cyril was my Principal. I come from a middle-class family. I have a sister who is teaching in the junior section.

When I was four, my parents decided I should be at Loreto, and I think that's the best gift they could've given me. The kind of exposure we get here I don't think I would've got anywhere else. When I go out to other schools and interact with other teachers, I've noticed they take a long time to make decisions, they are dependent on other things, but here we can make the decisions we want because of the kind of freedom given to us.

I teach Political Science and English and take care of the Catechism classes.

I think, we, the women, are the future of India. Do you doubt that we are the future? People have started to recognize this, giving women positions, and we are trying to make the most of it.

I am optimistic for India.

If you go back many years to when my mother was brought up, or her grandmother who never went to school, well, we aren't like that. In today's world, every family is trying to put their girl-child in school, and trying to see to it that there is no discrimination. I would not say everything is totally perfect yet—especially not in the remote areas of India—but in the cities, things are changing in big leaps and bounds, so I can say the future is definitely bright. People are becoming more aware of what the situation is, of what education is actually going to bring them.

When I talk about education I'm not just talking about education that helps you to get a job, where you are able to earn money and look after your family. Education is not just bookish knowledge. Education is something which helps you to become a better human being; where you think about yourself as well as others, where you grow not for yourself but for everyone around you. That is education, and that is the kind of education this school is giving.

I feel my mother's and grandmother's generation were kept behind doors and not exposed to certain things. As soon as my mother finished school she was married off to a person she'd never seen before. I wouldn't do something like that! Arranged marriages for me are absolutely fine, but only if I'm able to interact with that person, get to know the person. Then you know if your ideologies match or not, whether I'll be able to be happy with that family—I know there needs to be a lot of compromise—but I need to know if I can adjust to that family or not, and whether they will be able to take in the kind of person I am. In earlier times, people just got married and had to adjust; there was no way out.

One thing I tell my students is to speak what's on their mind and to not be fake.

At times, I feel helpless and angry because I can't do anything about certain things right now. In cases where women are being flogged in public, stripped naked and paraded around their village.

If I was in an important position, I could go out there and do something about it. I want to tell them they have the right to stand up and fight back, but I know the situation is very bad and dismal in the countryside right now. Sitting here in Kolkata it's okay to lecture, but down there the people are suffering.

It can be a simple issue such as a boy liking a girl from a higher caste, and her family goes down and starts beating the boy and his family and makes the boy rape his mother in public.

I tell my students, "You can't just say this is very bad, and then not do anything. Who is going to help? Who is the one to help?"

It is us who need to take up the reins, we have to speak our minds, we have to say we don't like it, and we have to go out and do something, not just say it.

Even if it's something small, we need to do it.

PART II

Thoughts on Education

The Enneagram: Who Am I?

To Run a Good School Is No Longer Enough!

Merit Is a Myth

What Is Education For?

Asking Questions

Management and Leadership

Understanding Children

Faces

"Barefoot" Teacher Training

THE ENNEAGRAM: WHO AM I?

Who am I? Who are you?

The Enneagram is a system devised by the Sufi mystics for the purpose of spiritual direction. It divides the human personality into nine categories.

Each one has what appears to be its own virtues but is also its vice.

The first type is the one that seeks perfection and is therefore always angry because they can never attain perfection within themselves or others.

The second seeks to give, to give the whole time, but does not want to receive anything from others and when their giving is not always appreciated they feel hurt.

The third one needs success. They detest failure, just as the first one hates lack of perfection and the second hates not being able to give. To attain this success, they're prepared to tell the odd lie and cut corners.

Type four seeks uniqueness. Nobody is like them, they're very special, nobody understands them. The most important thing for them is to not be understood. They are very artistic people, and no one can enter into their deeper feelings and emotions.

Number five seeks wisdom, but doesn't like to share it with anyone else. Very silent, they absorb everything, but they're worth listening to on the rare occasions when they speak, but they rarely do.

Number six is very loyal. They try to keep to all the rules perfectly, never break them, and in that lies their security.

The seventh type is happy-go-lucky and frivolous, they enjoy life, live on the surface, and don't go deeply into anything.

Number eights are strong, possibly bullies until they're converted. They're afraid of weakness, must never show it. But, actually they're quite soft inside.

And finally, number nines are passive. Their motto is that it's better to sit than stand, and even better to lie down.

I am type three. What it boils down to is how you deal with life before the age of five, back to the very earliest days and what we felt we had to do in order to be loved and accepted by the people around us.

In case of the first type, they believed, even as babies, that they would be loved and accepted by their parents only if they were perfect, and knowing some of these students as I do, I can see that their parents expected them to be perfect. The second type believed that unless they became generous and gave all their time to others, people wouldn't like them, and so on.

Looking back on my life, I was the youngest of three siblings—an older brother and sister—and all the time I felt I was measuring up and needed to be as successful as they were, otherwise no one was going to love me, although I was loved for who I was, but I never realized it.

The third type is competitive, and very, very early on I recognized this competitiveness within myself, and I put it out. I refused. Basically, if I want to win something, I will, but I'm very aware of it. If you look at my writings, I run the school on an uncompetitive basis because I can see how dangerous it is when it takes possession of you and everything becomes subservient to the competition and to you being first. Even as a teenager, I recognized that within myself, and I made up my mind that it was against my values.

You don't have to be in control. All you have to do is your best, and all the rest follows. If you have what it takes, you'll succeed, and if you have accepted yourself as God made you, what does it matter? That's part of my growth over the years, and the more successful I became and the more recognition I got, the less I did to strive and prove myself.

TO RUN A GOOD SCHOOL IS NO LONGER ENOUGH!

To run a good school is no longer enough. To run a good school in India, which ignores the plight and agony of children who are being totally neglected is not enough. We need to do much, much more! It's like the rich, young man whom Jesus told, "If you will be perfect, go and give all you have to the poor and come follow me," and the young man turned his back and walked away. Our principals don't want to give up their possessions either, their possessions being the good results they work so hard to get. If they admit too many poor children, they fear their results will go down.

And then what will the parents say?

They'll pull their children out of school, and who will pay the fees? The place will get dirty with all these poor children inside it, they say, and the teachers' lifestyles will be disturbed. They won't be able to go home at 4 o'clock and put their feet up and read the newspaper and watch TV, which means they'll have to stay on at school. And of course, if the poor children are living and boarding in the school it'll be even worse; oh, your whole life will be disrupted.

So, I say, to run a good school is no longer enough, because, we must, if we have a conscience, be looking after all these children who are outside and who nobody bothers about.

Look, I'm practical. Here, we're all practical. A lot of foreigners go out to places like Eastern Bypass, take one look at the living conditions and say, "Poor things, poor things." I say, don't pity them, do something for them!

It's no use crying about it.

Others come here with great intentions, thinking they can change the world in a week, but they can't. It takes time because you're not changing structures, you're changing people.

It will take time, and that's why we have to start now.

Outside of Loreto School, which has 1800 children, we take care of 30,000 others: 27,000 in 470 centres all over the city, another 2000 out on Eastern Bypass, and 1100 in the brickfields. And we will continue to take in more and more until the government gets its act together and starts a proper school system. When they provide schooling for all the students, I'll be very happy.

MERIT IS A MYTH

Merit is a myth. There is no merit.

You're either born with a lot of brains or you're not. And even if you're born with a lot but you're brain-damaged due to starvation when you're small, and you receive no stimulation from your parents because you grew up in a rubbish dump, where's the merit?

On one side is the child who has six tutors, and a TV and a PC at home, educated parents to look after every need, someone to polish his shoes and put them on, another to spoon the food into him while he studies for his exams. And having to compete with this is the little one down the road queueing at the pump for water, trying to get younger siblings ready for school because her mother's gone to make tea for the rich family at five in the morning.

So where's the merit?

Do you take the credit for your wonderful results, I ask schools.

Look at the clientele you're taking: Ninety percent of your good results is because of the home background. Ten percent you can claim.

But if you take a government school which takes the poorest of the poor, then ninety percent is the school's effort, and ten percent can be credited to the home.

"By their fruits you shall know them" seems to be the basis on which many parents try to choose the school to which they would like to send their offspring. The school with the highest number of first divisions is very often seen as most desirable, and no one looks at the background of the clientele, the basis of selection, the number of children forced to leave the school if they fail, and the huge amounts of money laid out on private tutors to "keep up the standards".

I often wonder, when I see the results of these other schools, how it is that Loreto Sealdah's results are comparable to theirs (even though we do our admissions by lottery so even our poorest have the same chance as others, and we take many children who have failed in other schools). Could there be some problem with their teaching?

This school was run on competition, until I did away with it over 30 years ago. Now, I find, when I read literature on education and what educators are saying out there in the world, that competition can be injurious to students because it distracts them from the task at hand, and it emotionally drains them.

If I simply prepare them to be highly competitive, stand on everybody else's head to get the best marks, it doesn't matter what they do to get them; they can even lie and cheat. Is that the kind of person I want to produce? No! Definitely not! Will that really make them happy? No!

We need to teach children that it is important to know how to accept failure and be able to realize that they're not going to be on top all of the time.

Many of Loreto's children have grown up in an environment of no competition, but they are so strong within that when they go out into the world, they know that the competition is not going to destroy them. Even if they do badly, they'll be able to shrug it off and start all over again. Whereas, you can train students up in a different system, and when things go wrong, their whole world collapses.

Competition is soul-destroying. The number of suicides amongst the young is increasing because of it. It is increasing because people see competition as the way to earn more money, and children's self-worth in school is often linked by teachers to their academic prowess. They are judged as good or bad because of their marks.

It's like the emperor's new clothes; no one is willing to say stop, where is this taking us? And unfortunately, we, as teachers and principals, are very guilty because we often fail to help parents recognize that their child is not a thing to be pushed and programmed like a computer. This is a person, to whom we must give time and space to grow. We must not impose our unfulfilled ambitions onto the children. I spend a lot of time with parents trying to get them to understand this.

If you're going to plant a little seedling on a street in Kolkata and expect it to grow into a tree, you'll need to put a fence around it, and you'll need to protect it until its big enough to stand on its own.

Then, you can take the fence away.

WHAT IS EDUCATION FOR?

What is education? What is it really for?

Of course, we want our children to learn the fundamentals, to ask questions, to have a curiosity about life, but beyond that, what is education for?

We need education so that all the children growing up in all the schools all over the world can become agents of change, who care about people around them, and who make sure everyone gets a fair deal. But you have to catch them while they're young and their hearts are malleable enough and have not become cold and stone-strong from all the things that are hitting them from every side. From there, we can transform the whole of society. It's possible.

Make them agents of human change, as opposed to violent change.

We have enough activists and terrorists around the world who all believe they're working for change, but what they're really doing is making a big mess. We can work towards a change in people's hearts so everyone can grow up not as a selfish person grabbing everything they can, but instead as part of the entire human race where everyone has a responsibility to everybody else.

To grow up in an interdependent society, not to take what they want and only use their power to get ahead and destroy others.

That is the meaning of Education for Community, and is what I introduced in Loreto Sealdah all those years ago.

Hopefully, this idea is spreading. Only yesterday, someone said to me that they were using our ideas in some of the bigger schools, older children teaching younger students who don't have proper schooling: "Each one, teach one."

In some government schools we've introduced small student teams who drop in at the schools and look after the students. Slowly, slowly, things are spreading out like ripples in a pond, each ripple creating another, giving hope that this kind of work will permeate throughout society. It certainly has in Kolkata.

I like the story of Johnny Appleseed, who travelled all over America scattering apple seeds everywhere. They grew up into apple trees, so any traveller along the way could help themselves to the fruit. He never went back to see what did or didn't grow, and I've been a little bit like that. I've gone around and scattered all these ideas, and they keep coming back to me in different ways, and I think things have changed as a result of that.

I gave a course on values to the teachers at a beautiful convent school. One of the values was love. So I asked them all how they taught their children love, and they told me they taught them to be kind to everyone and help others with their lessons.

Then I asked them about the slum that happened to be right behind their building. "Oh, that's a terrible place," they said, "the kids there keep coming over the wall and vandalizing our school."

"How do you teach your children love," I asked, "when you bus them into a big school like this, booted up and well fed, and yet you never challenge them to go over and take a look at the slum?"

So at my seminar, they made a resolution to take their senior students to the slum, and wrote me three weeks later to tell me they'd started an after-school programme. Children who would usually never stay behind to help were now teaching the slum children!

It seems like a little—nothing earthshaking—but if you change even one person's heart, you change something. It is not simply that we all have consciences and know these people are there and that all kinds of injustices exist, but to stir ourselves out of our busy lives and do something for people.

For me, that's the difference, that's the cutting edge of things.

ASKING QUESTIONS

If you keep asking questions, they'll finally get it. Students always do.

More than anything else, I teach the process of learning by arousing curiosity in my students so they want to find things out for themselves, and questions provide the springboard for that.

Teachers usually want to give all the answers.

I want more to give out what's necessary for them to think about, and to find their own answers.

Once students are literate, they can read their own textbooks, but I expect them to come back to me and ask a lot of questions, and check things with me.

What's the point in going over and explaining a textbook to them?

Isn't that an insult to their intelligence? Don't do that; they're too bright for that!

Children have good ideas.

They get their ideas not from sitting in classrooms and listening to two-dimensional teaching, but from exposure to real life situations with teachers talking to them, challenging them to think, to search for their own answers.

When I go around to schools giving courses, especially to schools with huge numbers—up to eighty or even more in a class—I find the teachers quite desperate, trying to cope with the numbers and the feeling that they have no time to reach everyone, as they have to finish the syllabus. Even when no one understands or remembers what they have taught!

When I suggest that they divide the kids into groups of eight and give them questions to work on in their groups, their first reaction always is, "They'll waste their time chatting." But when I finally convince them to work out a series of questions which cover the chapter and let each group tackle a different one, search for the answer and present it back to the class, they discover that, far from wasting time, the class gets really interested and comes up with questions for the teacher which enables her to actually teach the class material in a timely fashion.

It is important that children know that they can ask questions, even if the teacher does not know the answer. This is where the difference between the teacher who teaches from a fixed body of information and the one who is constantly open to new ideas becomes obvious. The response of the first will often be, "Get on with your work, and don't waste time," while the response of the second will more likely be, "How interesting, I hadn't thought of that before," or "I don't know the answer; let's see if we can find it together."

So the really good question is the one which leads to a certain curiosity and growth in one's capacity to think, and the really good teacher is the one who stimulates this.

MANAGEMENT AND LEADERSHIP

It has been said that many organizations are very well managed but very poorly led. This is because people fall into one of two categories. Either they busy themselves with doing things right, or they keep asking themselves "Is this the right thing to be doing?"

The first kind are managers and the second kind are leaders.

The manager makes sure that the status quo is maintained. Whatever was done last year will be done again this year! So the organization goes on from year to year with its t's crossed and its i's dotted, presenting the picture of a well-run, orderly and stable institution, an ideal situation when the organization has been designed to work with machines or some other form of industry and make money.

But if the organization is a school, dealing with the formation of human beings, it behooves the people in charge to keep questioning themselves as to whether the things they do and the rules they make are the ones best designed to fulfil the reason for that particular organization's existence.

A good example of this is a school which has mandated itself to become a resource centre for the poorest.

One of the poorest had two small children and was left with no means of survival when her husband died, except to send them around the wholesale market to collect all the vegetables and fruit which were thrown off the stalls because they were damaged, and bring them back to her. She then diced them up after cutting off the damaged parts and sold them in small bundles to other poor people who could not afford to buy anything else. In this way she could get enough money to feed her two children and herself.

Since these children were working from 6:00 to about 9:00 each morning, and school begins at 8:00 am, they would have been excluded if the school was following the "doing things right" model, as they could never arrive on time and had no place to wash or put on clean clothes.

On the other hand, since the school was constantly checking whether it was doing the right thing, these children were safe, as the school was flexible enough to adjust itself to accommodate them at 9:00 or whenever they came in and sensitive enough to provide space for them to bathe, wash their clothes and put on fresh ones.

In the process, of course, many t's would not be crossed nor i's dotted, but then this school was designed to cater to the poorest of the poor, so the person in charge was "doing the right thing" by creating an atmosphere and a space to cater to those on the margins.

UNDERSTANDING CHILDREN

First of all, I take children at face value, and I recognize that they may not want to always talk to me just because I'm an adult, not necessarily an authority figure.

If a teacher was not able to handle a student, she would be sent to me. My first reaction was always, "Tell me why you did those things." I believe that in many cases, children have a logic which we don't always understand, and they often do things according to that logic. If we stop and listen to it and see how logical it is, then we'll understand and we won't be punishing them, shouting at them for something that they did in innocence from their point of view. That has always been my rule for children, and very often, I've been surprised by the reasons they gave for doing something.

In schools, there are little bullies. Little bullies don't bully directly, they pass snide remarks that get under someone's skin—the Rainbow children are often the unlucky target—the little bullies find a weakness in one of the street kids' armour and they poke and poke until the child finally loses her temper and hits out. Then the little bully comes running to me and shouts, "She hit me! She hit me!"

My reaction is always the same. In front of both of them, I ask the little bully, "Did she really just hit you for nothing, or had you done something to needle her?" Usually the little bully has enough honesty to own up, in which case I tell her I'm not going to stand up for her at all, and I hope she gets hit harder next time!

Violence of the tongue can be much worse than getting hit. It can scar a child forever.

There are always children who have a strong sense of justice, and they're the ones who usually tell me when there is bullying going on. So I go up to that class and tell them I believe there is a bully in the room.

This is usually followed by dead silence.

Then, with a smile on my face, I ask, "Can the bully stand up so I can bully her?"

Nobody ever moves.

I tell them we've now established that the bully is a coward, and so in the future, when you see bullying going on shout, "Coward, coward, coward!" until it stops. I usually give the bully a second chance to stand up and be brave and admit it, but they never do.

There are, no doubt, reasons why people bully. The bully often feels very insecure within, so when they feel they have someone they can lord it over, they do.

But whatever their reason, it's the one thing in life I have the most utter, utter contempt for.

FACES

I do this exercise in my Courses for Teachers.

I divide the teachers into eight groups, and assign each group a picture of a differently shaped face: square, round, rectangular, triangular, diamond-shaped, frilly little amoeba-like shapes, and so on. I cut each picture into eight parts, and distribute the 64 pieces randomly around the room. Then I tell the groups to find the pieces of their "face" and make it whole again. That's the only instruction I give them.

Many of the teachers sit and look at me for some time. I don't speak. After a while, some of them move, and then gradually more do, then they begin to share ideas, and when each group has made its picture whole, they all come and sit back down with me.

I ask them, what was the first thing they needed in order to make the picture?

All sorts of reasons are given out, before they tell me: Move, we had to move.

As teachers, nothing is ever accomplished unless you move. God told Abraham to move out to a land that He would show him. He didn't say, come along, I'll take you by the hand and show you.

You have to move first, take the risk, then you can be shown the way. This is the way, of course, in which you, as teachers, can live your own lives. Move out from your safe positions, take risks, look out and open your eyes, and make yourselves alive to all the new things out there.

I continue questioning them:

"Did you do it in silence?" I ask them. "No, we talked," they say.

What happens in classrooms?

Some schools you walk into are dead silent, you hear nothing but teachers' voices, and many teachers tell me this is good; it shows a school full of respect and discipline. But I think it shows a dead school not functioning well, asleep. If you want absolute quiet and discipline, go to a graveyard! Teachers look at me with wide-open eyes, and their principals even more so, because they suddenly realize exactly how their school is.

To make any of this work, you need a noisy school.

I'm asking teachers to reflect what they do when they work in these groups, and why they work in groups, and what they need in order to work together as a team: communication, cooperation, perseverance.

Then, at some point in the faces exercise, we come to the teachers' groups that have been given the triangles and diamonds. All the other groups with the easy circles and squares have long finished, but the triangles and diamonds are easily confused, so these groups are still on the floor, fighting over bits and pieces of paper. I tell the finished groups, sitting around like smug cats, that they must be the brightest. "Yes, we are," they agree.

And to the groups still on the floor, I tell them they must be the slowest. "No, no, we're not," they say, "we're not slow!"

Ha! What do they learn from this?

There are no slow learners!

It's just that for some people the pieces are confusing and take much longer to put together. And this will always happen, since some students learn differently.

So, why are "faces" chosen for this exercise? Our faces are the means by which we know everyone and understand what's going on.

Students look at a teacher's face wondering what kind of day they are going to have: a good one or a horrible one. Everything shows on your face. There might be a child whose exercise book was torn up by her younger brother, who then came into school late and was punished. How do you handle that?

Your children's faces will not tell you any of the above; they will simply accept stoically and take the blame.

We, the teachers, need to become sensitive to these children in the classroom, especially if our other children are well off, and do not need such empathy.

"BAREFOOT" TEACHER TRAINING

Young children don't like learning a lot of stuff from textbooks which have no real meaning for them. They learn best from things they're familiar with and which they enjoy. Therefore, while they can be forced to memorize everything, the process is long and unpleasant and very damaging, especially when the child lives close to nature and has to attend school in a stuffy room with meaningless symbols on a page, when the whole textbook of nature lies open and inviting outside the window.

However, if the child's natural desire for play is channelled into methods of learning, and her interest is stimulated, she will learn much more, much faster, and be motivated to work on her own.

That's where "Barefoot" teaching comes in. "Barefoot" teachers (Shoes aren't necessary for walking, feet are!) are young or older persons, who have failed in Class 7 or 8 and are more likely to remain in their villages or slum areas, where unfortunately, their education isn't put to good use.

And yet, these people are a precious resource, because in their communities they are often the only ones with some literacy. If they are given even basic teacher training, they can become very competent teachers at the primary level. They understand the local situation and are willing to teach in remote areas where the "qualified" teacher will not go, and quite often get support from the villagers/slum dwellers, since they live within their locality.

In fact, this system really benefits the first-generation learner, as no help from home is necessary since the child learns at her own pace, and the teacher observes and records her progress on a day-to-day basis. This removes all strain from the child and leaves her sufficient time for the all-important activity of play, which strengthens her body and challenges and stimulates her imagination and creativity, which in the twenty-first century will be her greatest asset.

It also leaves time for the tribal/village child to work, which is important for her family's survival.

The Barefoot Teaching Programme involves more than providing education at low cost to indigent people. It aims to restore to communities the right to educate their children in a way that suits them, and to help them to act instead of depending on others. It is an attempt to correct the narrow specialization that has come to be associated with learning, and the high costs that make schooling prohibitive for those who need it most.

We've been running these courses for many years now, and there is such a growing demand that we have a waiting list. Interest is growing all over India. The government has now expressed its appreciation of the programme, as it is a very cost-effective method to provide education for the poorest and most neglected children, especially girls. So, at the moment it looks as if it will take off as a sort of movement.

The courses are conducted throughout the year at Loreto Sealdah, along with a follow-up over a two-year period. Our team goes out to teach in the field in between the "at home" courses.

Everything is conducted in the language most suitable to the trainees, that is, Bengali, Hindi, English, and training covers Nursery up to Class 4, including planning lessons, making teaching aids, and guided teaching practice.

We recently introduced the concept of science teaching at the primary level through simple experiments. Extra training on leadership and community development, and training in working with women are also available.

Our latest development is the training of trainers, who have gone back to their villages and collected potential teachers and even government teachers. Having such people in the field means that monitoring is easier, as short courses can be taught frequently and then followed up.

In India, with a quarter of a million villages, each with its own local government—and probably another million clusters of hutments not worthy of inclusion in the statistics—the options for poor children, other than a life of exploitation, are virtually non-existent.

Our low-cost training in modern child-centred methods of teaching, using the environment as a textbook, makes education a reality for such children. Even those who are slower to develop will acquire, in the course of three or four years in primary school, the necessary basis to either join a government school after Class 5, or to be a better farmer, tailor, fisherman, etc., later on.

We have very positive feedback from the trainees, many of whom have started teaching under a tree! This has the added advantage of enabling curious parents to participate also, as they gather around to see what is going on.

If the trainees continue to be as enthusiastic as they are, we may very well have an educational revolution on our hands!

INTERLUDE

AN IRISH JOKE...

Paddy was accused of stealing the widow Murphy's pig, and the parish priest said to him, "Paddy, listen, many years from now when you die and go to the Pearly Gates for your Last Judgment, God's going to stop you and say, 'Now, Paddy, you tell the widow Murphy here what you did with her pig.'"

So Paddy asks, "Father, are you telling me that the widow Murphy will be there right by God's side?"

"Oh, yes, the pig and the widow will both be there to accuse you of what you've done."

"Well, then, I'll say to her, 'Widow Murphy, look no further. Your pig's right here!'"

EDUCATION

...is acquiring skills and knowledge

...is developing values and learning to live by them

...is learning how to adapt to new situations

...is learning how to relate to others

...is learning how to cope with problems and seek solutions

...is learning to make decisions based on a God-given value system

...is acquiring the ability to take responsibility for one's decisions and actions

...is preparing to take one's place in society and to contribute positively to improving its quality

...is ensuring a prestigious career for oneself

THE OFFICE MANAGER

I have been married for 38 years and was married at the age of 18—a love marriage. I won't say that was the first boy I met; I had met many boys before, but somehow we fit together. He's not very handsome to look at, but I was much in love with him. So, still now, I have that feeling, after 38 years living together—happy, our children settled down, three grandchildren, and still we're in love.

I still look forward to weekends—I have a day off tomorrow—and I look forward to it, and he does too. He never says to me, "I love you," but it's in his actions, the feeling. He becomes very happy when I'm there, so I don't usually go out on weekends unless he's with me. If I get an invitation for myself only, I usually don't go. And I've got my mother-in-law, too—she is now 80, and I know she wants me in the house more. She never demands that I have to stay, no, it's not like that; we do have a nice relationship. I'm like her daughter. Our love is not in words but in our actions and deeds.

I came to Loreto in 1977; it's like my second home. It is my second home; the office here is never empty. I leave my house at half past seven; I'm here by 7:40, depending on the traffic, and school starts at 8:00.

I have done this for 33 years.

I'm here at school until 3 o'clock every day, but because of Sister Cyril we are all very flexible [laughs]. I try and finish all my work within that time and if not, I carry on until it's done. But she's also been here for many years, since 1979, and I've learnt a lot of things from her. Before that, I was working as a secretary in an office in Kolkata.

Ever since Sister Cyril came here, there has been so much social work, and Loreto has grown so much that I don't think we can ever finish all our work. My nickname is "the Administrator", and Sister Cyril depends on me as I depend on her. When she's not here, I look after the administrative part of the school, and us and the teachers mutually benefit from each other too.

And since I've been here for so long and I'm Bengali, many of the parents—90 percent are Bengalis—approach me, and I translate for Sister Cyril if they have any problems with their children—and there are problems—and the problems are sorted out in front of all of them.

I can do whatever I want here, like it's my own house, like these trophies and prizes here on the shelves I bought last year when Sister Cyril was away somewhere else [laughs]. It's like a showcase, and I like it very much.

This place is the children's home as well; it really has a lovely atmosphere. There is no difference between the rich and poor students, no feeling like that, and you can approach anyone at anytime for anything. No one thinks, "Oh, she's poor," including the children from rich families. Their parents know this, too. In fact, compared to other schools, I can really see how independent our students are; when they finish their schooling here, they really shine. Many other students I know in other schools continue to depend upon their parents, very mollycoddled and all that, but here, the girls become very strong and can think for themselves.

My daughter studied in this school; she's a teacher in Delhi now, and her daughter is still here. She could easily have put her daughter in a good school in Delhi, but she didn't because whatever values she got from here, she wants her daughter to have, too.

PART III

Thoughts on the Students

The Rainbow Children

Confidence

Giving It All Away

The Alumni

Jayna

THE RAINBOW CHILDREN

From the age of ten and onwards (Class 5), all students have two periods per week called "work education," which is compulsory and where they are expected to use their hands in some way: book binding, tailoring, sewing, woodwork, skills they can use later. But here in Loreto Sealdah, what better "socially useful productive work" can we have than to go up to the roof of the school and teach whichever Rainbow children are there.

The Rainbow children go through a programme when they first arrive here: a base-line test for reading, writing, literacy, and then they are put into a suitable level. If they are ten years old, they should be ready for Class 5 within a year, by being brought up to that level and helped by the regular students.

If the children are younger, we can put them straight into our English-medium classes. If they're older, it may take longer than one year, but they will eventually be placed in school. But they're not kept in the Rainbows indefinitely, as it is only a channel in which they're prepared by the regular students.

Everything they teach the Rainbows is written down in special files with a format: date on which they were taught, what was taught, how much was taught. So, from day to day, as different classes come up and take over, they can check the records and continue the work.

All classes (even our ten-year-olds) get the chance to do this work. EVERY CHILD teaches and passes on her skills to help the street children, who in turn are quick to learn. This accelerated learning, now promoted by the RTE Act (Right to Education), has been happening in our schools for many years.

Not only do our students have to teach, they're often the ones who go out to rescue the street children and bring them into the Rainbow programme. In many schools, they have very good social justice and human rights programmes, but there's no hands-on experience going on, and unless there is hands-on experience, especially in India where children grow up cheek by jowl with poverty, the students never see it. That's why I make them go. It's only when they see how people live in places like Eastern Bypass, smell the smells, or see the atrocious conditions in the brickfields that they can get involved, that things will change.

We have to push them out there to recognize it all for what it is.

Another reason they go instead of someone like me, for instance, is that if I have to go to the Red Light District, the people there say, "Oh, Sister's come, here she is." And I'm this great, big, fat lump dressed up in my nun's habit, and it's all so obvious to everybody. Whereas if we can send people who meld into the background, then we're more likely to find the truth. That's how we find out who to bring into the Rainbow programme.

Every now and again, the Rainbow children get fed up with the general organization of the place and they start doing what they like, coming down for lessons whenever they feel like it, dropping banana skins all over the place, all that kind of untidy behaviour.

Once, there was a big plate of food left over by someone under the cupboard and it had begun to smell; oh, it was horrible. So I made every child smell it. Then I told them, unless I find out who left it, they will all wait for breakfast tomorrow until I arrive (a time gap of thirty minutes). So, the next morning, they all waited the extra thirty minutes—of course none of them owned up to it! Then we sat down and had breakfast. I told them I didn't want to see a single crumb or anything on the floor. Everyone finished in twenty minutes, and I told them all to stand there and see to it that the place was spotless, then I gave them all a sweet each, and told them let's see what happens tomorrow. The next day, they were perfect.

When the children are first rescued and brought into the Rainbow programme, they are closely questioned: who they are, what kind of family they have, information about aunts, uncles, brothers, sisters, and their case studies are written up. It's important for us to know their backgrounds. We visit the families of the students who are very poor, under the poverty line, those who will need to have certain concessions. All this is discussed with them, so everyone concerned knows what is in store for the child. Only certain members of the staff have access to all this personal information.

I've noticed, over the years, children return to us when they're in trouble. We might not see them for years until there's a problem. That is significant. They know where they can get help, and they trust that the help will be given.

When fights break out and girls come to me and demand justice, I tell them to keep standing there looking into each other's eyes, to not look away for a second, because it doesn't matter how angry they might be with each other; if they keep looking at each other, they'll start smiling. And when they begin smiling, I ask them, "Would you have been so angry if she was your best friend?" "No," they say, "I wouldn't have been angry."

"So," I tell them, "your problem here is not what was said to you but your relationship. If you're friends, it wouldn't matter what you say to each other. But if you're not friends, you feel it and you get hurt."

CONFIDENCE

One reason for our students' articulateness and conciseness of speech is that from the age of ten, they have to teach, they have to hold the attention of twenty wild little village kids, and express what they want to say in such a way that those children can learn something. This helps to build confidence within them that makes them believe that they can speak. They're also expected to get up and speak during Assemblies.

When I travel to other schools, colleges and universities in India, only a few students are articulate; many are not. A lot of the education imparted is out of books. You sit, write your exams and get a very good result, but it doesn't allow you to stand up in front of an audience and speak. The general run of education is not designed to develop children's verbal skills. Most children sit in straight rows, and are not allowed to talk to anyone in class. The teacher teaches; the students listen and put it all in their notebooks.

Whereas our crowd here seems to be unable to shut up; everything you say to them has to be said over their voices, and discussed and argued. Unless I blow my whistle. But that's a simple convenience for me, because it allows me to control them when there is something important to say, and I only expect them to be quiet when there is something important to be said. They're not expected to walk down the stairs quietly or stand in Assembly in dead silence for the sake of discipline. Discipline, to my mind, is a very misused word!

I'm always thinking of ways of selling all of this to other principals. It's not just one-way traffic whereby you send your students out to villages, and then you bring in all these street children to mess up your place. Your students get back a lot more than that! They get more back than they give, and if you ask them, they feel it too. I've never taken a group out of here to a fancy, independent school, but if I did, I don't think they'd be out of place.

In these youngsters, there is a depth you won't find in children generally—you'll find something else but not this kind of depth. Loreto students are not self-conscious; they're coming from a non-competitive system which means they are only ever expected to measure up to themselves, to better their own performance and not to worry about anyone else. The result is when they get up to speak, there are no overtones in them of trying to be better than the other children. They are relaxed in how they perform, and more focused on simply doing it. No one is comparing them to others.

We keep collecting all kinds of materials on everything we find: global warming, environment, evaluations, anything we can find so the teachers have constant access to what's out there.

For example, in our groups of thirteen-year-olds, we have a reading range of between eight and twenty-two years of age—up to a post-college level—so the teacher has to be aware of their capacities in class, and if the range becomes too wide, they will need to be separated.

Is this radical stuff or just common sense? It's common sense to me, but within the Indian scenario, where few follow this system—even the big schools won't do it—it allows their teachers to not teach too well in class so the student must go to them for private tuition. I know one very well-known boys' school where the Master of Chemistry came into class, wrote his name and telephone number on the board, and said, “You’ll need to come to me in the evenings for help; you won’t be able to do all of this by yourselves.”

Where does that leave the poor child in that kind of set-up? Students can get pushed out of that kind of school very fast, so while the people at the top have the best of intentions, they need to know what’s going on in the classrooms.

GIVING IT ALL AWAY

I got the chance to take a group of Loreto Rainbow senior girls to Holland. We had lunch with the middle school children of a big Dutch school, and they left a lot of food over and our girls stayed back to help clean up. They objected very strongly to all the food being thrown out, when so many children in India had to go hungry, and the staff were amazed at their awareness of issues.

Later, my students were given 50 euros to go and buy themselves something nice and some presents for their friends. So off they all went, and when they came back later, they gave me back the 50 euros.

We couldn't waste the money, they said, we couldn't buy anything to take back because the money translates to about 3000 rupees which could feed so many people in India.

Our trip was sponsored, and we were staying in various hotels, so the girls collected all the soaps and shampoos and all the other complimentary items the hotels gave out every day. All these were brought back to India. Then they sat down for a couple of days and concocted some beautiful little parcels which they decorated themselves along with thank you cards they made, and those parcels were handed out to everyone who had helped prepare them for their trip.

And one last thing: they had also been given boxes of sweets and Dutch chocolates, and these they broke up to put inside their parcels. They took nothing for themselves.

It was amazing, and I was perfectly happy. It showed the character of the girls and I felt proud of them. They made a fantastic impression in Holland, the way they spoke to people and made presentations for large fundraising groups. Those girls were the first fruits of the Rainbow programme.

When we first started, the Rainbows used to go out and get hold of the leftovers of chicken and bring it back, saying, we got it for nothing, nobody wanted it, and we can boil it and make some lovely soup.

Nobody else would look at that kind of stuff.

They made bargains, going around to buy shoes for each other to go to school in, very conscious of the cost and the need for thrift. This was the character of those who came off the streets in those early days, and we see it in our children even now.

THE ALUMNI

The alumni are very smart in the sense that their eyes are open, they see what has to be done, and they go and do it. Many of their employers have said the same thing. They don't stand around waiting to be told to do something, they use their initiative.

One alumna comes from a family of four girls and one boy, whose father was earning 300 rupees ($5) a month. The five children were almost transparent, so we always made sure they were fed at school. She grew up in the school itself, and later, she came back looking for a job, and at that time I needed someone to look after the Hidden Domestic Child Labour Programme. I'd already connected with a number of schools around Kolkata as to where the child labourers were employed, and I gave the list to her.

The first thing she did, without my saying anything, was to organize the postal codes so that when she came to employ people for a Save the Children project—which funds her to this day—she could contact and employ all the girls who would have been considered also-rans, girls who didn't do very well at school and who were coming from very deprived backgrounds. She has about twelve to fifteen of these girls working with her, and they are outstanding.

Another girl got a special prize when she was thirteen for caring for one particular little boy who was a domestic worker at a tea stall. One day, he spilled a pot of boiling oil and burned himself from his waist down, and she was put in charge of him. She took him to the hospital, got the right medicines for him, visited him every single day to check that he was being properly looked after and explained everything to his mother. Later, he was completely cured. She is still employed by the programme and works in one of the slums in Kolkata.

Another older alumna got married and moved to Bengaluru, where she worked for seventeen years in an IT company and now has enough money to work for herself, so she decided she'd spend the rest of her life looking after poor children and giving them opportunities.

Many of the Loreto alumni display the same kind of intention and awareness. When they leave school, there's a period when they experience different things—maybe they aren't helping the poor, but they don't feel guilty about that—and yet, many of them return to social work later, after their studies, saying, "I've established myself, I can give time to other things, to helping people."

What makes these girls such a powerful group is that they're empowered from the minute they come into school. The first rule I ever made was telling their parents not to carry their young daughters into school, not to carry their water bottles and books for them. All the girls were expected to do things on their own, and a sense of responsibility was encouraged.

We used to organize groups of children from overseas to meet up with our students. They would all sit down together and share their views on life, and what struck us all was how articulate the Loreto girls were compared to the visitors. They can express themselves so well about life, the news, what's going on in the world—everything really—and it's not just a few select ones, it's all of them.

It's the same thing when they are sent out to competitions. We had a rule that once you've been to a competition you don't go again; you stand aside and let someone else go for the experience. We made it clear we were happy for them if they won and equally happy if they lost. We never sent them to win, but sent them for the experience.

When you see others win, you learn what made them win so that you can then practise it yourself. So even girls who would be considered below average elsewhere would be allowed to develop into something very good. Many schools send the same students to win every time because they make the institution look good.

I never bothered with things like that.

JAYNA

Jayna is eleven years old. She's a long, lanky girl, who looks a bit like a fish, and she is very bright. She came to us with dreadful behavioural problems—no one else would keep her; the children's home simply wasn't able to hold on to her.

When she first came to Loreto, if she didn't get what she wanted, she'd take off all her clothes and run around naked, screaming like a wildcat at the top of her voice, so we had to control that first. I would catch her by her shoulders and hold on tight. "Calm down, close your mouth, calm down, calm down," I would say very, very quietly. "If you stop, I'll listen to you."

It took at least two months' work until we could talk and listen together.

Then we sent her to school, but she did no work, never studied at all, so she failed Class 5. She'd already failed it before in her other schools, because she was running around the whole time, it was impossible for her to sit still. So we had her do Class 5 again, but she was still very disruptive, running out of the class when she felt like it, and the teachers finally begged us to take her out of school.

So I put her with the Rainbow children, and let her do whatever she wanted for three months, no questions asked. Then I sent for her. "You have all the Class 5 information in your head," I said, "even though you didn't listen, but you're like a computer, so if you're willing to sit down and do one subject at a time for Class 5, then do a two-hour test at the end of each subject and pass, you can go on to Class 6, and Class 7 next year. Do we have a deal?"

"Yes!"

"And one more thing. If you need to get up sometimes and run around the yard to use up some energy and after come back to my office (it was holiday time, so I had told her she could sit in my office) then do it because you'll feel better." So she did.

She passed her Bengali test, and took every other test for each subject and passed. One of the other girls, a friend who is quite brain-damaged but who has come through by sheer perseverance, offered to sit beside her in the tests and keep her company.

After the tests, Jayna told us very strongly she wanted to begin studying in the English-medium classes. "If you want to do that," I explained, "you'll have to go all the way back to Kindergarten and start all over again and be in class all day long, and if you run away from class, we'll take you right out of school, completely."

We kept her hanging on for about a fortnight. She went to one of the older girls, a mentor, and told her how we were always threatening her with something whenever she did anything wrong, and she didn't really think we were going to put her into the English classes; we were just saying that so she would stay in class. All this from an eleven-year-old!

I called her bluff, and put her into Kindergarten—she could read a few English words, but no more, and she couldn't really understand what she was reading—but she mastered the books very rapidly. Within two weeks she was in Class 1, and two weeks later the teacher told me she was too advanced and put her in Class 2. Over the next six months she moved up to Class 5, sat for the unit test and passed, and that November she cleared her exams and was promoted to Class 6 with a medal for progress!

But, she still has to learn to accept it when we say 'no'.

She is improving, she's starting to do the "house duties" that she's supposed to do, like all the others, and she is trying to listen when the other girls ask her to do things.

I've got one further hold on her; she doesn't like to have her hair cut. If you make trouble, I told her, two officers will bring you to my office and we will cut your hair. She went wild, very defiant, and was so strong it took three of us to hold her down. We cut a tiny bit, enough to give her a tiny lesson.

Afterwards, I sat with her for a long time, holding her hands, quietly saying over and over, "Calm down, calm down, calm down." All the tension went out of her. She had first come to us without any real medical history, but we were pretty sure she had been placed on prescription drugs before to keep her quiet, and you can't do it that way.

She has learnt over the last couple of years that we will give her justice, provided we can hear what she says, but she has to calm down and state her problems clearly, and only then will we listen. We will not always let her have her own way. That's why when she tells me she doesn't want to work with certain teachers and will go off some place else, I tell her, no, she'll stay right where she is and work and go where I put her and nowhere else.

A while back she would have screamed and stomped off at this and refused to go to class at all, but now she's more reasonable; she's enjoying English-medium classes and doesn't want to give it up, and by next year, I can guarantee she'll have the ambition to go the whole way. She also knows she's being helped by the other girls around her who speak English, and I tell her, say whatever you want first in Bengali then put it into English so you can speak it. She picks up fast. She's very bright, oh my God so bright; she has everybody taped, she knows exactly how far she can push us.

There isn't much that can motivate students like Jayna; there's no challenge for them. But she needs help to get over the desire to get her own way all the time. When she goes out to work later on, people are not going to give her her own way, so she has to learn that and accept it.

Recently, she rescued a cat and presented it to me. She adores animals, although earlier she had inadvertently killed two kittens—squashed them with love. So I thanked her and gently took the cat from her before she could squash this one, too.

INTERLUDE

AN ANIMAL JOKE...

A very kind, elderly man found a lost penguin and decided to bring him to the police station.

"Don't bring that in here," an irate police officer said. "Take it to the zoo!"

So, off the old man went, and two hours later, there he was back again at the police station with the very same penguin.

"I told you to take him to the zoo!" yelled the police officer.

"I did take him to the zoo," the old man explained. "But I was wondering where I should take him next: the cinema or a museum?"

FOUR STUDENTS AND THEIR DREAMS

A: I want to be a journalist, a media person.

B: I have a dream to study law; I'm not sure if that will be successful or not.

C: I also want to be a journalist. After graduation, I want to do English Honours, History, or Sociology—I've got three options. English is my first preference, let's see, then after I complete that, I want to go into Mass Communication.

B: India is still developing, it's good to be here, it really is, I feel proud to be an Indian—we all feel that way—it's a very diverse country... religion and culture ... and there is unity in that diversity, and whatever it is, it is our country and we belong, so I'm bound to like it.

A: There is trouble here, of course, there is political turmoil, but still we have unity. For example, we may work together for the betterment of other people, and I consider that to be something. If you are considerate to work for and help someone else, or your country, that's good enough.

C: Change is inevitable for us. Change, yes. Hopefully, it will all change in a positive manner. More people will be educated. Poverty is a major thing in India, and that will go down if people like us are working—ha, I'm so full of myself! India will be more developed industrially, economically. We worry about terrorism, of course, and illiteracy, child marriages, child labour, and we hope in the next twenty years, India will be devoid of all these things. We hope for the best.

D: We love London and all its history, but we wouldn't want to study there, no, we want to study here in India. I want to work for India. Money doesn't much matter to me. People who have patriotism in their hearts don't need money.

PART IV

Thoughts on Social Issues

Mosquito Nets and the United Nations

The United Nations' Millennium Goals

Charity vs Development

Microcredit

Justice

…And Injustice

The Environment

The Future, Our Future

MOSQUITO NETS AND THE UNITED NATIONS

One of the things I remember from the United Nations in 2003-04, was that they were busy giving out mosquito nets in Africa. Each net was made in America and cost about $2 or $3, and my first reaction was, "You big fools! If people in the West want to help, send money." The Africans don't need rugby balls from Australia made in China! Anything they need, they can make themselves over there. And provide employment. Why import them from abroad?

I'm a practical radical.

If I ran the UN, what would I do? I feel like the Irishman, and the Englishman says to him, "How would I get to Ballyjamesduff?" and the Irishman says, "Now if I was going to Ballyjamesduff, I wouldn't start from here..." Well, I wouldn't start with that great, monolithic building they have, no, I'd start with the top of their list of Millennium Goals: "Make Poverty History."

You won't make poverty history by manufacturing everything in America and shipping it over to Africa. You set up industries in Africa, and you pay equitable salaries. I'm not an economist, but I do know if you have as much money as the UN has, we should not spend it on sending envoys around the world in first class transportation, and have them stay at 5-star hotels!

What about the salaries they draw? I'd cut down on all that kind of expenditure so there is more money to be given to the poorest of the poor. I would also put stoppers on the money on its way down from top to bottom because at each level, in developing countries, a cut is taken by various people.

How do we deal with that?

Education, motivation, and care of the poor; it's always those things.

I'd stop the schools where children are being taught to hate. If we teach children how to hate, we're asking for trouble, and there are large swathes of certain communities that are being taught to hate. It's not that the whole community wants it, no, it's just a few fanatics, and then everybody gets tarred with the same brush.

I would abolish ALL guns, and make it a criminal offence to make a gun, anywhere in the world.

No guns! No landmines! All totally forbidden!

Go back to bows and arrows and personal combat. If you want to fight someone, get at each other, eye to eye, hand to hand. If the governments won't educate for peace, then let us do it ourselves, and let it spread out in ever widening circles.

THE UNITED NATIONS' MILLENNIUM GOALS

1. Eradicate extreme poverty and hunger
2. Achieve universal primary education
3. Promote gender equality and empower women
4. Reduce child mortality rates
5. Improve maternal health
6. Combat HIV/AIDS, malaria, and other diseases
7. Ensure environmental sustainability
8. Develop a global partnership for development

These goals have constantly been held up before us to be achieved. But how much of the world's population is concerned?

We are all aware of the enormous gap between what should be done, what can be done, and what will be done, a gap which is caused by our innate tendency to continue in a straight line until forced to stop or change direction. And there are two such forces: one is our conscience, when we take time to reflect (it doesn't always work), and the second one is the law (not so good, as it implies coercion). But they are all we have!

The more we reflect on the ills of the world, the more we realize that education is the answer, but not, and I have said this already, an education which promotes competition but one which prepares children to build community.

An Indian lady crossed the border into Pakistan with a group of Indians on a friendship mission. She approached a Pakistani soldier on the other side and told him, "I lost my son to a Pakistani bullet on the border." He put his arms around her and said, "I will be your son."

Community.

MAKE POVERTY HISTORY/ERADICATE EXTREME POVERTY AND HUNGER

Sometimes I see the world as a huge ant heap with all the ants rushing about their business in all directions, all so preoccupied with what they are doing, so isolated that the idea that they could cooperate to achieve anything together seems very remote. And yet look at the ant hills they create! All built by thousands of ants, each bringing one grain of mud.

Unfortunately, we humans are not ants, and so we will have to be reprogrammed differently, to stop being so busy about our own affairs so we can pause long enough to see the needs of those around us. When a twister hits Oklahoma, or a tsunami drowns Southeast Asia, we are all shocked to silence and everyone rushes to help. But once the immediate need is over, we drift back to our own lives and concerns.

If we are to make poverty history, we need to become as single-minded as the ants, each of us bringing our little grain of mud to build a new society where there is (as Mahatma Gandhi once said) enough for each one's need, though not enough for each one's greed.

How to start?

With our students, we went out to Eastern Bypass to speak to the dispossessed people of the area. They said, "Give us schools for our children." So we said, "Have you anyone we can train?" So they gave us four girls and two boys, and we trained them in how to teach and to do a survey of their needs down along the railway tracks. Our students each gave up a day of their school holidays, and we sent out twenty of them every day, each with a pack of twelve dice and some letter cards, and in the month of the holidays the street kids learned to count, to add and subtract and to recognize their letters.

We trained the teachers in basic methods, which they taught to the kids in the morning, played with them in the afternoon, and did adult literacy with the parents in the evening. As soon as they were ready, we introduced microcredit, and now they are able to run their own small businesses and make their own profits instead of being in the hands of moneylenders and middlemen who exploit their skills for a pittance and grow rich on their hard labour!

One grain of mud towards the ant hill! Come on, all you other ants, let's work together!

ALL CHILDREN IN PRIMARY SCHOOL

Such an obvious goal and yet so many children all over the world are not being sent to school, are in child labour, or child armies.

In India, the RTE Act (Right to Education) was finally passed and became law in 2009. It concerns itself mainly with school infrastructure, which, in a country where the best of education was imparted under a banyan tree in ancient times, has sadly shifted the emphasis once again to appearances, rather than concentrating on a high level of thinking and problem-solving, a really quality education which would benefit the poorest and most neglected children. In an effort to get such children ready for school, we have been privileged to share with the Government the material on accelerated learning prepared by our teachers. As part of our "ant" activity, our Class 8 and 9 students have been trained in their use and have passed that training on to others in the Government schools so that all over Kolkata, children are searching for those who are still not in school and persuading them to come in.

It will take a year or two, but our ants are working...

GENDER EQUALITY AND EMPOWERMENT OF WOMEN

Microcredit, preceded by literacy and the dignity that goes with it, has been the single most important factor in moving towards the empowerment of women. Of course, it is understood that men must achieve literacy along with women, but we confined our microcredit to women, and it has worked out well. Education of girls is very important, but it must be such as to give them the power to fight, like the family I found at Moulali (a crossroads near the school) on the side of the road at midnight, all upset and crying because their father had come back drunk and beaten up their mother and them. I was angry as this had happened before, so I loaded them into their rickshaw (which I had given to their father to earn a living for the family) and got someone to bring them back to the school.

They stayed on in the Rainbow Home, and later on when they were older, they went out themselves and confronted him about his behaviour and forced him to give up the drink—absolutely unheard of in India for schoolgirls to stand up to their father in this fashion. Here's to the power of education! And the empowerment it imparts.

REDUCE MORTALITY RATES IN CHILDREN AND IMPROVE MATERNAL HEALTH

These two goals are closely linked and need to be addressed very early in every girl's life, in fact from the time she is born. In most poor families (and in India, all families) the boy is always provided for first, and yet it is the girl who will be responsible for the nurturing and development of the next generation. In this context, food and education for the girls become imperative, as does breastfeeding, which is nature's way of spacing the children. So many NGOs are working in this area, but until we have a massive change in attitudes towards women we will not get far. At the same time, it is not so long ago that women did not even have the right to vote, and even now in some parts of the world they are still very much second-class citizens. But changes are happening and rapidly, even though we must do more!

REDUCE HIV AND OTHER DISEASES

Children are powerful purveyors of messages to the local community and, through their parents, to even further reaches. As schools we can surely inform our students on the effects of HIV, malaria and other diseases which are ravaging so much of the world. I was in South Africa a few years ago, and they told me in all the schools I visited that not more than 30 percent of the children were being reared by their parents. The majority were being looked after by grandparents. I wonder how much population will be left in Africa after a hundred years.

HELP SUSTAIN THE ENVIRONMENT

One of the reasons sustainable living isn't working is because people are not involved. It's not inside of them. They are living a certain surface life, and as long as it's comfortable they will continue doing the same things. Only, only when things become uncomfortable, when it's their house that is flooded, or their town that's threatened by wildfires, or their kids who are threatened by new health risks, only then will people change. They have to become more aware, they have to suffer, things have to hit them before they move.

The same thing is true for children. We have students who come up through school who get away with doing the bare minimum work required to pass and keep going, and suddenly, around the age of fourteen or fifteen, life hits them between the eyes, and they realize if they don't do their best, they're stuck. So they put their heads down and do marvellously well. They begin to gain more insight, and they change.

If our children can do it, then we can do it, too.

DEVELOP A GLOBAL PARTNERSHIP FOR DEVELOPMENT

We need to leave building partnerships on a macro level to the nations of the world. But micro-level partnerships are easy for schools, and have been happening over the past twenty-five years in Loreto Sealdah, and have spread to other schools and other countries, as the concept of service learning has spread more widely. Many groups of schoolboys and girls from opposite sides of the globe have worked together to address issues of development designed to improve some real situations of need. The involvement of our children is crucial, and the happy memories they carry with them of these exchanges mark them for life. Who knows, but maybe someday they too will join the ranks of those who make the decisions on which so much of humanity depends! I think of Gandhi's reply to Nehru, when he asked him for advice on how to be a Prime Minister. "Think of the poorest and most deprived citizens, and ask yourself how your decision will affect them, and you will not go far wrong."

CHARITY VS DEVELOPMENT

There are two ways of helping; your help can make people dependent or it can make them independent.

It's easy to give out charity. Several groups do a nice programme, but all of it is based on their particular business, so they kill two birds with one stone: yes, they give to the poor, but they sell their own things in the process. It doesn't really benefit people other than the fact that they get a handout.

The best way is to educate people so that they can stand on their own two feet, or provide them something to start off with and then they pay it back and continue on without us.

The problem is that most charity doesn't involve people. If you are given something you haven't made, something you haven't had a hand in, you'll be less likely to use it well. In many teacher training courses, the whole kit is handed to them by the Government—everything printed up and nicely laminated for them—and wherever you go in India you'll find them all locked carefully away inside cupboards so the children won't spoil them! Whereas, what we try and do with our teachers is to give them a template, which the teacher can then refer to and prepare new things to suit new situations of learning.

The minute you do it yourself it becomes yours. You will use it, and you will remember it.

In Malda, the groundwater is about 12 feet below the ground, and the villagers couldn't easily access it, but the land is very fertile, so every village was given a diesel pump to pull the water up. But no one taught them how to look after the pump, so when it ran out of petrol, they filled it with water.

Hundreds of absolutely useless rusty pumps lie in the fields simply because nobody trained the local people how to use them. And when you're dealing with local people who are not schooled, how would they know what to put into an engine?

We have to listen first. We have to sit down with them and find out what their real needs are.

That's the difference between development and charity. In India, we should develop people, and they will develop the resources. The mistake the government keeps making is continually developing the resources but not developing the people to look after them.

In Lolay, there was a terrible shortage of water and they had to walk to the top of a hill to get it as that was the only outlet. So, one of our Sisters went to her hometown and talked to them about the villagers' need to tap their water, and her parish put their hands in their pockets and gave her lots of money.

She returned to the village, but she was wise enough to consult the village elders first, who said, no, no, they didn't need taps, as they didn't mind walking up the hill for the water. "What we really need," they said, "is tin roofing for our houses, because every year we have to grow straw with which we thatch our roofs. The land for this is being used wastefully, whereas we could grow crops on it. So if we can get tin sheets for our roofs, we won't need to grow straw." So she got the tin roofs installed, and the result is that the land has now been released for cash crops. If she hadn't asked them, they'd have all been given taps they didn't want.

What I've learned is to become much more sensitive when you help people, work with people.

You go in as a servant, not someone who is arrogant and trying to tell them what to do.

If you have a servant, and tell him you want toast for breakfast, he doesn't turn around and say, "No, no, you don't want toast, you need cereal." Can you imagine how long he'd last?

But that's exactly what we do when we help people. We decide that you need cereal, not toast, when we should actually be asking them, as humble servants, what is it they need?

If we listened more, more would change, yes. People would work with you, not just sit passively and receive from you.

That's how I see development.

See the problem, look at it together and struggle on it together to produce something new.

I may bring something to it, you may bring something to it, but the problem gets solved because of our combined efforts, not because I come in with all my answers and all my money, and tell you to do it my way.

That's how the World Bank and the big corporations behave.

They manipulate to have it done their way. That's why I don't accept money from the big sponsoring agencies because they tell you what they want. They give you a budget for clothing, outings for children, private tuition, but what I want are fees to pay my teachers with. I want money for food so the children can study properly. These are always my two big needs, but they're not to be found in their budgets, because their money is so tied up I can't use it for the things I really need.

They don't listen, and no one's ever forced them to listen.

I like to be free.

MICROCREDIT

I went to a conference in north Wales in 1986, and someone asked me what message I wanted to give people. Help people find solutions to their own problems, I said, don't give solutions, but assist people in arriving at them. Let them do as much work themselves as they possibly can.

Microcredit is a fantastic tool for development. We began here, in Koli market, with some of the parents of our children. They were buying stuff wholesale in the market with borrowed money and losing it all back to the moneylenders, because they had to pay a heavy interest on it. But as a result of microcredit, most of them have made enough money to rent for themselves a small room where they can keep their children.

We've had no bad debts. Almost all have repaid their loans. We gave out the equivalent of $5000 in September 2008, and 97 percent of it was paid back by March 2009. They are charged 2 percent interest on the money we lend them, and they pay back on time because they're women.

Indian men tend to drink the money, so they can't be trusted.

Women can be trusted because their family is at stake, and that is their first priority.

They have a sense that they have been helped in some way, and if they can give that back then they can help other people, and so they can be helped again. What is important is that community feeling.

In Eastern Bypass, they've set up 8 companies of 12 people each, and all of them are producing, so they want to expand and have already got their recognition from the government without any help from us. A similar group of women at Madhubati started with help from us and have already received their first grant from the government. The beauty of development is that once people are launched, they can carry on by themselves, and we are released to provide the same support to another group.

JUSTICE

What is justice?

Is it where you treat everybody absolutely equally, or is it treating everybody according to their needs?

The law says you treat everybody equally, and if you go into a Court of Law, it listens to everyone's reasons, but it doesn't necessarily treat everybody equally.

Two men walk down the street and both of them stab somebody. One gets off with manslaughter, and the other is hanged for murder.

Is that justice?

It's because each man has a different motivation, and the law digs into that motivation.

It is the same at school. Children come to school late but for different reasons. One is just lazy, won't get up when her mother calls her, dawdles over her breakfast, is driven in her big chauffeured car, and is late through her own fault. Another one lives in a hovel, has to dress and wash her younger brothers and sisters, has to find them all something to eat, and when that's done, comes to school hungry.

If they're both late, should I treat them both the same?

What would they learn?

For the chauffeured one, cutting up vegetables in the kitchen or scrubbing down a few walls is usually enough punishment to drive the lesson home.

But for the other one, I'll just tell her to go up to class. (Of course, I'll give her something to eat first. I wouldn't send her to class hungry!)

I might even have a third one come in and tell me her train was late, and I say, "Look me straight in the eye and tell me the truth. Was your train late, or did you get up late?"

"...I got up late."

"Fine. You told the truth. Go to class."

I have told my children to come to school, no matter how late, even if they can only make the last hour. They will still learn something, and they can find out what they have missed.

When I first came here the children would bring a letter from the Station Master if the train was late, and would spend thirty minutes waiting for the letter. So I told them not to waste their time, that I'd believe them if they told me, even without proof. When people are treated fairly and know that they are trusted, they usually respond by becoming trustworthy, and children reared on trust do not forget.

...AND INJUSTICE

Within families, especially in poorer families, the father eats first, the boys eat second, the girls eat third, and the mother eats last, if at all...

Where's the justice in that?

Where's the justice in some families—especially patriarchal ones—where the parents do not want the girls to work outside the house, even though the girls might well have been sent to a good school?

I can recall many instances; the mother who came in to see me with her two sons, who were both being sponsored and had reached Class 10, and then I discovered her daughter was a former student of Loreto and spoke perfect English and I asked the mother why her daughter doesn't get a job at a call centre. She told me they didn't want her working outside the family, and yet she had no problem coming to me and asking for money for her sons to finish school. Why doesn't she allow her daughter to earn money in a respectable job and put her sons through school? The mother had no answer to that.

Over the years, I've had many families with children who have been educated by us come to me literally starving because of this problem.

The daughter is prevented from working by the father because she's a girl. Simple as that. If she had been born a male, she would, of course, be sent out to work. A girl must be protected within the family in case someone gets at her. Isn't it strange to assume that on any given day, every girl could be a target of every man on every street?

The biggest injustice of all here is bringing up girls with minds already pre-programmed and caged, and the girls themselves don't want to fight it; they accept the strictures because that's the way it's been.

The irony of it is that if they're well educated, they become better marriage material, and the family doesn't have to pay such a high dowry. And if they get married into a more liberal family, the husband and the mother-in-law will see the girl as a means of income and allow her to work.

In this case, the girl is no longer a liability to her own family.

Unfortunately, if the girl is raped before marriage, nobody will want to marry her because she's "used material," "impure," "secondhand." Rape is seen as something terribly dishonourable, and usually the girl is blamed. So, if the family can get her married off quickly, the danger somehow is less.

There are so many other forms of injustice: we were trying to collect the government cheque from the Treasury and cash it on time. I sent a bearer down to them a week before the deadline, and she returned to tell us that their clerk was demanding 30 rupees to collect the cheque. This made me angry, so I wrote a note to the Head of Treasury telling him what had happened, and he told me to see him at once. I've always found that the higher the office you go to, the quieter things get, the deeper the carpets, the cleaner everything is. We told him the story, and then he told our bearer to try and cash the cheque again while he observed. She was rejected once again by the clerk, who was subsequently transferred to another department where he wouldn't come into contact with the public.

I calculated, if on the final day of every month the clerk was processing 7000 cheques and taking 30 rupees each time for himself...!

This kind of injustice is the one that everyone suffers from. People like me will fight it, but it's difficult for poor people to do so because they have no clout. I do. I can go straight to the top man but others can't, and that's where justice will probably be given, not in the middle of the pecking order.

At Loreto, we give the girls enough energy to fight all of this. We teach them that when their mother tells them to get up and fetch a glass of water for their brother, they should tell him to get his own, that it's much better for him to do it himself.

It's not just the girls who have to deal with injustice, but the mothers as well. In India, the business of men beating up their wives is endemic, it happens in many, many families, including the rich ones.

To get into the good, larger schools, boys start learning how to read and write at two years of age and get hammered across the knuckles if they don't do it right, and I believe by the time many of them become teenagers, there is a high level of anger within them. Anger like that doesn't find an outlet until it finds a victim, someone who can't fight back. I know of many very well placed men in society here who get drunk, go home and beat up their wives. Of course, it is something that is repeated in other societies all over the world.

For many years, I had to put up with a local councillor who was always pushing me to take new admissions into our school, and we, in turn, were always asking him to fix the hole in the road outside our school gates that would fill up with water every monsoon. "We fix your pipe, you take this child," he would say to us.

One time, I could take it no more, so I wrote him a letter telling him if the pipe was not fixed by tomorrow, I would take all my young students and leave them standing in their socks in the waterhole outside the gates. It was mended very quickly after that.

The rules should be the same for everyone.

Recently, there was a fight outside a college, where one student shot at another, and a policeman got in the way and died. The lady chief minister refuted this version and instead said the killing was done by a member of the Congress Party (one of the main political parties in India), and that he should be arrested. The police had the whole incident on video and arrested the young student. The Chief of Police was then summoned by the lady chief minister, who told him to change his story, which he refused to do. She promptly demoted him to serve as her own personal bodyguard, which he refused by telling her he intended to take some time away to look after his sick mother in Delhi.

The lady in question here might not hug me so quickly next time we meet.

THE ENVIRONMENT

Our school has a special club for the environment, and every class now has environmental studies, but there is very little in the syllabus about cleaning up after oneself. This is something which should start in each home as soon as children can toddle. If there is a container, and children are taught from a young age to pick up after themselves, perhaps we can improve. Until the homes begin, it becomes a school responsibility.

I always insisted that our children clean up after themselves. When we had our annual fête, no child was allowed to go home until everything was cleaned up; all the desks and chairs put away, all the rubbish swept away and put into bags, while the parents stood patiently waiting until all was perfectly clean, and applauding, asking us why they couldn't get their children to do the same at home!

We held several competitions for a Cleaner Kolkata, organized by the *Telegraph* newspaper. Our students put up posters all along the road outside school, where it is particularly dirty. They gave out bins to the different shops, and for a while, the place was transformed. It was interesting to watch the shopkeepers look after the bins for the children, and nobody defaced the posters along the road; our side of the city looked very different from the other side. Yet, once the competition was over, everything went back to what it was before.

One of the reasons there is so much dirt in this city is the fact that the city corporation cleaners sweep everything up into nice little piles at the edge of the road, but the collecting lorries come on another day, by which time the local population has kicked it in all directions! It's not well-organized, to put it politely, and sustainability is in short supply.

I was teaching a course at a local Bengali school, where all the local Brahmin families sent their orthodox daughters, and I told them they should all sweep their own classrooms. There followed a big furore over this because when they tried to implement it, the teachers wouldn't accept it, because they were all Brahmins, too, and they felt Brahmin girls shouldn't do this kind of work. But when one of the teachers actually began sweeping, all the girls crowded around and joined in, and it became a local event, which continues to this day.

The only answer is to EDUCATE.

Natural disasters are only a disaster because of the way in which we have built and constructed things, without any reference whatsoever to the nature around us. If while constructing we took cognizance of nature, we wouldn't be in the mess we're in now. I do believe that.

In Darjeeling (a hill station north of West Bengal), houses are built on stilts into the hillsides, and the slightest rain can disturb them. On the road south from Gangtok (a town north of Darjeeling), engineers have bored into hills to build a dam on the river for hydro-electricity, and all they have succeeded in doing is totally polluting the river. There is little or no awareness or cognizance of nature whatsoever. We ignore it, and we face the consequences of having ignored it.

I've found there is always one important element missing in construction projects such as these: how to make the work meld into the landscape so as to become part of it.

The indigenous peoples who occupied these lands before we came along to put up all these buildings would have a lot to teach us about this. The tribals here in India have lived for centuries in perfect harmony with nature but have seen, since Independence in 1947, many of their forests sold to Big Business, who then moved in and cut down all the trees. If the tribals so much as touch a tree, they get punished. There is a tribal group that is, at present, fighting with a large coal mining company, which wants to destroy all their arable land and much of their forests to make way for a local mine.

I'd like to get into the minds of these people who are determined to go ahead with their coal mining. Why can't they see anything other than the short-term? Why is money the only thing they ever think about? Don't they care that they're ruining things forever?

I'm also very interested in the use of water and how much of it we waste. Do you keep the tap running when you brush your teeth? We give no thought to how much we waste and where it all goes. I ask children to do an energy budget and to keep an eye on how much electricity they use at home, and how much of it their family wastes. We need much more understanding of all this.

Industry is using and polluting tremendous amounts of water.

I wonder if we'll actually run out of water, or that certain areas will and others won't.

In Kolkata, the water-table is sinking, because so many people have sunk tube wells and are pulling their water up directly from the ground. Because all the roads are concrete, how does the water get back down into the ground to replenish the water-table? We need to create more open spaces where water is able to do this. There are huge bodies of water all around the city but they are being filled up by large high-rise developments, and so when the monsoons come, the water has nowhere to go and it floods. All the excess water runs into the sea and is lost.

Save.

Live frugally, as we used to.

There are many people out there who want to change things, but we need to save, and drum it into our children to do the same, who in turn, then tell their children. That much, I know, we have to do.

SAVE.

Long ago, we didn't have so much, but now, we have so much stuff that we take it for granted and don't treat it with respect.

And if it's there, we'll just use it until it's gone.

THE FUTURE, OUR FUTURE

We have to take collective responsibility for the future, and we have to stop blaming each other for the past.

In our programmes, even in the most difficult places—out on Eastern Bypass, in the brickfields—wherever we work with people, it works. I've seen it. It works.

It was funny, watching all those people getting up at the Bill Clinton thing at the United Nations, and pledging to prevent so many millions of tons of carbon being sent into the atmosphere. And so on, and so on. Then someone from Ethiopia got up to say the amount of carbon and pollution his country put out was minimal, and then the Indians explained that even though their collective breath of 1.2 billion is enormous, their carbon footprint is also tiny. The whole thing is so unequal, so there's no way you can make a standard law for everyone.

First of all, people need to stop and think.

I am not defending India at all because we are very careless over here. But slowly, slowly, an awareness is coming, and I don't feel we're any less aware than people in America who have two or three cars, who drive a few blocks to drop their children off at school. Some schools have even told their children not to run to school, because a fall might become a claim for compensation. Can you imagine the level we have reached? So silly.

We have to change our way of proceeding with each other. We need to learn how to give. We need to realize that our salvation lies on the level on which we're prepared to give.

You make your choice between prosperity and destruction, that's what it comes down to, and we have to make up our minds.

I mean, what was the Copenhagen Accord all about? Did anything happen? No. They drank a lot of good coffee. They couldn't come to any kind of solution because they're looking for a solution in the wrong direction. For them, it all comes down to money and economy. Nobody wants to give up anything because it'll affect them and their whole lifestyle and their capacity to enjoy themselves.

It all has to become less.

Climate change creeps up on us so slowly, it doesn't make a big impact on us, so we feel we don't need to change. It's such a slow process until it actually happens, but now it's speeding up, and it's reaching a critical mass. Whatever is changing, though, is not so strong as to make us do something about it. When a black cloud of pollution comes rolling up our street, affecting us, affecting our children, then, yes, we'll get upset, then we'll react. But right now, we still can't see it.

We can't quite see it... And when we do, it may be too late, like the absurdity of Ireland not having enough grass for its cows because it was so cold the grass did not grow.

That's our whole problem. I don't know what will happen.

And it's late, it's getting very late.

I saw a diagram showing that we are in the last ten seconds of the world. Terrifying to look at it, if you believe it, but we don't believe unless it hits us straight in the face.

A man was thinking he might or might not give up smoking until his doctor told him he had cancer. He gave up smoking.

Until it hits us...

I am always seeking some way in which I can get past people's inertia and reach them at a point where they will actually do something, and it then becomes an insight for them. Nobody ever changed because they made resolutions. You change only when you get an insight that hits you.

It's like that.

Damn it, do it.

Yes, it's like that.

Damn it, do it!

INTERLUDE

A MONASTERY JOKE...

This monastery had a cat, and every day at 6 o'clock, at morning prayers, the cat came in and disturbed the monks. So they resolved that the cat should be tied up at 5:55 every morning so as not to bother the monks at their prayers.

Time went by, and the cat died, so the monks went to great lengths to get another cat so she could be tied up at 5:55 every morning so as not to bother the monks at their prayers.

More time went by, and people began writing learned treatises on the meaning of tying up the cat at 5:55 every morning so as not to bother the monks at their prayers.

And so on and so on and so on...

THREE STUDENTS AND THEIR WORRIES

A: Our street outside the gates is very noisy and very polluted. It's dirty, which I don't like. I want it to be clean. It's in the middle of the city, the traffic makes it difficult to cross the street, but it's convenient as it's on the main road.

When we look at our school we feel happy we've got our rights, like good education, but I feel sad for those who haven't. Everyone has rights but some are deprived of them.

When I walk through my school it's depressing that a child outside cannot get sufficient food and studies, and I want to change that, and I think I am getting the opportunity here to do that.

Our parents encourage us to feel like this and not just sit back and watch.

B: Global warming increases pollution, which damages our health. And water pollution, deforestation—we need to hold rallies against this, spread the message of not cutting down trees.

C: I feel corruption has increased in the world, which is creating destruction and the death of common people. Terrorism is also increasing, and global warming, and it must be stopped in some way. The world is going nowhere but towards a life of death.

TYPES OF FEAR

True education is a process of liberation from the fear which prevents a human being from growing to his full potential–spiritually, intellectually and emotionally.

The fear of:

Thinking independently, lest we make a mistake

Expressing our ideas, lest we be laughed at or criticized

Speaking before others, lest they disagree with us

Saying what we really think, lest we lose the good opinion of others

Refusing to conform to the group, lest we be rejected

Making any move first, lest we be wrong

Being ourselves, lest people take advantage of us

Giving others responsibility, lest we be blamed for their mistakes

Standing out from the crowd, lest we be singled out

Being relaxed, lest people think less of us

Trying out something, lest we find we can't cope

Asking ourselves why we do things, lest we find out something about ourselves we do not want to know

PART V

Thoughts on Religion

Mystical Experiences: How Big Is Your God?

Creation

Meeting Yourself in Silence

Faith and Religion

Life and Death

Violence in the Name of God

Conversation in an Office
(interview)

MYSTICAL EXPERIENCES: HOW BIG IS YOUR GOD?

God's mercy is infinite, but many people don't really believe that. God's here with us all the time, but for many, God is just a word. We have all these lovely mandates and rules and messages. We talk about it all the time, but are we actually doing anything to make a difference?

No.

I don't expect God to do my work for me. He's given me a free will, a sense of responsibility, a pair of hands, a good brain, eyes and energy, which He hasn't given to some other people.

I'm one of the few Christians that He has in India, but I keep telling people that if He really wants the whole of India, the whole of Asia, to become Christian, then He should have put a few stronger instruments here other than the likes of me!

I doubt that He wants everyone to be Christian.

If you consider the saying "Love your neighbour as yourself," which is what my concept of Christianity is, you will find many people doing just that. But they are people who really believe it, don't just pay lip service to it, but live it out and challenge others likewise.

When I was in Canada, I met the Mennonites, a group of Christians who put the Gospels into practice literally. One couple had been visiting a prisoner for twenty years every Sunday because he had no one to care for him, even though the jail is several hours from their home. They followed what Jesus said, "I was a prisoner and you visited Me." I ask myself, have I done as much?

How big is my God? How small is my God?

There was a woman of 97, whom a priest had gone to visit, and he asked her how she was getting along.

"Well," she said, "I'm just waiting to go back to God, and ask Him to forgive all my sins."

All this woman could think of was how small her God was. After 97 years of serving Him faithfully, she was still bothered about the sins she had committed, as if God was counting them all up!

My God is so big I can't even imagine Him. He is a very, very, very, very big God. He's the God of the universe, He holds every single atom, and He's too big to be bothered about all the little fiddle-faddles that I do and all the times I've lost my temper. I tell him I'm sorry and all that, of course, but I don't think He's too concerned. But He's very concerned when I've lost something and He finds it for me, or when I have some big projects to finish, or some poor person to help.

When these kinds of things happen, He becomes a smaller God with a big vision who can see everything and can provide all that's needed. I get total support from Him, and I believe He does everything, through me. He's there and involved with me all of the time. He walks and talks with me the whole day long. I wake up with Him, sleep in His presence; He's there all the time.

All the things that are written in books, we believe in our head, but they don't always show in our actions. That's because we don't really, really believe them.

Many people who believe in God just say the words and their prayers and amen, and that's it. They just go through the motions. You see the children here doing it all the time.

The only thing you have to remember is that God is inside of you. Just be there with Him. That's enough.

I discovered this many years ago on an eight-day retreat. On one particular occasion, I was praying, when suddenly there was this terrible cracking noise. It was as if all the paving stones on the Loreto Lucknow veranda were banged together at the same time. Then it went very quiet, absolutely silent, and I heard this voice say, "Be still, and know that I am God," and in that moment, I knew I was to just shut up and sit quietly and be in His presence. He didn't need me to say anything, or read the Bible, He didn't need anything.

And now, often, when I sit down and open the Bible, something in me says, put it down, put it away, it's you I want, not the book.

So I sit and keep myself there for Him. You don't need anything else. Don't distract yourself. Don't read anything. Don't do anything. Don't say anything. Just sit.

It's not always easy.

On another retreat in Darjeeling, I was sitting asking God to come and take possession of me when I felt this terrible pain, as if God was tearing at me. I suddenly saw how shallow I was. I was the shallowness of a tin can turned upside down—if you look at the bottom of a tin can, the rim is very thin—that was my shallowness, and I realized I didn't want to be shallow like that, I wanted to be deep. So, I was resisting this tearing, but no, if this is the depth You see in me, I thought, then so be it, I accept it, and straightaway, it was like a big SHOOOP, He flew into me, like that. Father, Son and Holy Spirit.

So, when I talk about God, I'm talking from a lived experience. People may say, it was only a psychological thing, but what I felt was absolutely real, and many, many others have had these kinds of mystical experiences as well.

What does God look like to me? Nothing. He's just there.

When I meet people of other faiths around the world, I certainly don't have conversations about God with them. We talk about the work we're all doing now, in the present.

I have a Leadership Training Service group who have been with me since their student days. The group gathers for prayer to discern what

God wants them to do in society, and they ask me to take a morning of prayer with them, every now and then. I play some music for them, then I ask them if anyone would like to drop a line, a phrase, a thought into the silence. Then we share a prayer, and we come together at the end to share where we are in our life's journey back to God.

Simple as that. We never go into philosophy or anything like that, as I don't have any interest in the different philosophies of the different religions. As far as I'm concerned, God is our common father, and we take different paths, but He's there and we go to Him, and are inspired in our lives.

CREATION

The seven days of creation happened exactly the same way for evolution.

Those time periods and the order in which they appear all correspond to the way evolution actually happened.

A week is a period of time in the Bible; it doesn't literally mean seven days.

Before any human beings came along, what was the meaning of a week? It could have been an eon of time, taking millions and millions of years to occur.

You don't have to be so literal about it all.

Within me, I find both the scientific and the spiritual can live and work very nicely together.

So, when I see a cat, or a dog or any other animal, I am always struck by the beauty of God who designed them. Even looking at the sky early in the morning or just after a monsoon shower, the air is so clean and fresh and the colours so bright.

How beautiful God must be, how deep all His mysteries.

Even now scientists are only discovering how a lot of what we see around us really works, and in some cases it is too late, things have been damaged beyond recall, species have become extinct, and once that happens all our much-vaunted progress cannot recreate them.

I often like to read books about Nature as it was some hundreds of years ago before anyone came into the picture and spoiled things.

How did those living so long ago get everything they needed from Nature without destroying it, as we seem to be doing? Our education is not geared up to help explore how best to live with our environment.

I wonder how God feels having to see us damage so much of His creation.

There is only one consolation. If even a stray twig is left, it will begin to sprout and put out leaves, but what is so sad is once an animal species is extinct, we have no means of bringing it back.

And we don't seem to realize that we are the losers!

MEETING YOURSELF IN SILENCE

Silence is important so we can get in touch with our inner selves, but children are rarely exposed to silence these days. In my childhood, there was a lot of silence: picking primroses, looking for bluebells, walking in the woods. There was a quietness, a kind of gentleness about life. Nowadays, in cities like Kolkata, there is never a moment of absolute quiet. Always a horn blaring, someone screaming, music playing somewhere.

Many of our children live in noisy high-rise flats, fifty families almost living on top of one another. So, I try and get the children to find these quiet moments inside themselves.

When I teach them prayer, one of the things I tell them is that the one time they are sure to be left alone is when they're studying.

Their parents will be so thrilled that they won't want to bother them! So that's the time to find quiet.

Each child should have their own testament on their study table—if you're a Christian there's the Bible, if you're Sikh you have the Guru Granth Sahib, Hindus have the Vedas and Bhagavad Gita—and when you sit to study begin by opening your scripture and simply ask God, "Do You have a message for me today?" Then read slowly, and somewhere along the line something will strike you, so pause and stay with that, let it deepen. Then move on quietly. Do that for five to ten minutes, and then get on with your studying.

This has a tremendous effect on them. Try to do it every single day, I tell them, it's a simple thing.

This is one way to help them find their way through this jungle of noise. If you have constant noise the whole time and you've grown up with it, how do you ever meet yourself? You don't! Many of our young people are afraid of silence, so it is important that we help them acquire a taste for it early.

If anyone comes to me and asks "What's the point in trying to meet myself?" I say, "If you do, you'll become much deeper, much happier. You can get to know yourself and be happy with who you are and bring balance and joy into your relationships."

Some years back, we introduced a two-hour yoga session once a month for everyone, including the Rainbows. I was amazed to see 500 adolescent girls sitting in perfect silence following the instructions of the yoga master and telling me after they finished that they felt refreshed!

Around the same time, during a Prayer weekend in Ireland for young people aged 17-25, I sent them out in silence to find God around them in nature. I later found them behind haystacks, smoking, chatting, doing all kinds of things! I said, "If you want to go out and find God, go alone, don't talk to everyone out there! Who are you fooling? Me? God? Yourselves?"

They sat looking at me, and said they'd never been asked to find God in silence. The retreats they had done in the past, the priest would talk and talk and talk, and they were told to just sit and listen, all the time supervised by the teachers. But no one ever explained the reason for silence and the need for it if we are to reach God.

I see it in the schools everywhere in Ireland. There is not even a remote understanding that children could be asked to calm down. No one tries it with them. They don't give them the chance.

I think this is one of the great gifts India has for the West—to bring back this element of silence into people's lives to enable them to meet God on a daily basis.

FAITH AND RELIGION

Historically, people came along who were inspired by God to start a movement back to him. Each of these movements has gradually, over the years, become a religion, developing its own unique rules as any organization does.

But in all these religions, God is supreme, above everything else, and we all make our way back to Him on our own particular path. I believe Christ is the way back to God, but my common sense tells me He's not the only way back. Whenever possible, I preach His values—I don't preach Christianity itself—but I do that best by living those values in my real life. I don't believe just preaching them gets you nearer to God.

Besides which, I do what I can, but I can't convert people. They have to be converted by God's spirit inside of them. He is the only one who should bring people back to Him.

Spirituality is distinct from religion. Religion can become an extraordinarily empty ritualistic thing, and for many people who have stopped going to Mass, it's because for them Mass is no longer a life-giving activity. They're not meeting Christ at Mass. That was why, when we held our first Friday Mass at Loreto Sealdah, my idea was that after Holy Communion there would be no hymns, no loud singing, none of that kind of carry-on at all, but rather a total, deep silence with yourself.

Go right inside yourself and talk to Him. He understands from the inside, He knows all your strengths and all your weaknesses and your faults, and He still loves you no matter what. Go and speak with Him.

Spirituality is where we really meet God and we can do that outside of all that ritual stuff. The ritual is important in that it brings people back, face to face with God, but unless you have got your relationship right, it can lose its meaning.

I've noticed people get frightened of conversations about religion. They can't handle it. They can hardly handle it if you pray in public.

I was in New York at that big hole in the ground created by 9/11, and a man walked up to me and said, "Sister, will you pray over me and bless me?" I said, "Certainly," and I put my hands on his head and blessed him, and the nuns who were with me said, "What are you doing?"

"What's wrong?" I asked.

"You actually pray in public over people?"

"Yes, of course, if they ask me," I said.

What's wrong with that? I thought. They were embarrassed.

Most people in the West are embarrassed by religion. In some places in America, they won't even allow you to mention God. I once gave a talk there at a public school, and I was warned that I must not mention God. But the truth is that same school had kids on drugs, and all kinds of blasphemy going on, but no mention of God.

India is the exact opposite. India is a secular society, but we recognize the right of every single religion to have everything according to its Gods, and for people to have the right to propagate or change their religion. All these rights are recognized and all religions are seen as equal.

India has a tremendous message for the world; you can have people living together, and still everyone does their own thing.

LIFE AND DEATH

For death, people use expressions like, "She's expired." "She left for better pastures." You go back to God and then you're happy ever after if you've behaved yourself, and hopefully he's merciful if you haven't.

When we die, we go back to God. I haven't given my mind too much to thinking about when I die. I think I'll lie down and relax totally, totally, totally, and let my spirit go back to Jesus, and I'll simply move out and leave my body behind. I read that we go down a narrow passage, and there's a blackness and then a light at the far end where we emerge into this beautiful place with this gorgeous feeling of being loved and cared for.

But for me, it'll be when I meet God face to face, and I hope He'll say:

"I was hungry and you fed me,
I was a stranger and you took me in,
I was a foreigner and you visited me,
I was poor and you educated me."

Come blessed of my Father, possess the kingdom prepared for you from the beginning of the world. That's what my hope is. I don't have any other hopes.

I'd never say to Him I did my best, no, because if you say that, it sounds like you're saying, "I did my best, so now you can look after me for eternity," that's something I won't do. Because He knows inside I've not done my best. He knows how much I could possibly have done if I had stretched myself, so for me, to say it in front of Him and shake His hand so I can enjoy eternity, well, that sounds terribly cheeky.

Maybe I have lived a wonderful life. I've certainly led a very enjoyable one, and I've got the most out of everything. I've loved peanut butter sandwiches with bananas and crunchy nuts, ice cream, and driving the car and playing basketball and swimming and tennis and reading lots of storybooks.

All the things I shouldn't have done, I've done, so I don't think I've had a very difficult life. I've never gone in for great penances, I've hardly deprived myself of anything, so I certainly wouldn't consider myself as having had a tough life. I enjoy what I'm doing, and when you enjoy what you're doing, it's not tough, it's more like a holiday.

VIOLENCE IN THE NAME OF GOD

You can have people fighting and killing each other over religion, but in truth they aren't fighting for God at all, they're fighting for themselves.

They don't really believe in God; God is a God of love, and every religion is telling us to love our neighbours.

If you're fighting with someone over your religion, then sorry, you're not fighting for your religion, you're fighting for your opinion.

That is very different.

What is it that makes people fight? What's telling them, "My religion is better than yours!" It's an ego trip. True spirituality removes the ego, there is none, and we're focused on God as the only important being for us as well as our neighbour, because God inspires us to do that. We won't be busy trying to be better than someone else.

I think we're all the same. It's that simple. The same, but we all have different ways of looking at things and our different ways of meeting God, but that's all because of programming when we were young.

If we were all born and left to grow up without this programming, I don't think there would be any difference. The differences are artificially created by our upbringing, family and culture.

When the Rainbows first started to come and live in the school, a fight broke out one night. I found a group of Muslim girls fighting with a group of Hindu girls about their religions and festivals, and I can still remember sitting down with them all and saying to them, "Look, you're all here. Most of you have no one outside to care for you, you're here now. So what difference does it make whose religion is better? We're all going back to God, we all have our different paths back to him, that's where we'll all end up, so why do you have to fight along the way? You have to live here as sisters, so sit here and think about it."

If you're fighting, you're not a religious person at all, whether you're Hindu, Muslim, Sikh, Jain, Buddhist, Jewish, Catholic, Protestant or anything else, you're not religious.

You're defiling God by pretending to be His follower, and then contravening the most sacred of all His lessons to us: you love the Lord your God with all your heart and mind, and love your neighbour as yourself. This do and you shall live.

That's the whole thing, it's as simple as that. And if you go through all the great religious scriptures, you will find the same message coming through, couched, perhaps, in different idioms, but clearly telling us that LOVE is what God asks of us and not just for our friends but for our enemies as well.

Baha'i Faith Lay not on any soul a load you would not wish to be laid upon you and desire not for anyone the things you would not desire for yourself.

– Baha'i Faith, *Gleanings*

Buddhism Treat not others in ways that you yourself would find hurtful.

– The Buddha, *Udana-Varga* 5.18

Christianity In everything, do to others as you would have them do to you; for this is the law and the prophets.

– Jesus, *Matthew* 7:12

Confucianism One word which sums up the basis of all good conduct is loving kindness. Do not do to others what you do not want done to yourself.

– Confucius, *Analects* 15.23

Hinduism This is the sum of duty: do not do to others what would cause pain if done to you.

– *Mahabharata* 5:1517

Islam Not one of you truly believes until you wish for others what you wish for yourself.

– The Prophet Muhammad, 13th of the 40 *Hadiths of Nawawi*

Jainism One should treat all creatures in the world as one would like to be treated.

– Mahavira, *Sutrakritanga*

Judaism What is hateful to you, do not do to your neighbour. This is the whole Torah: all the rest is commentary. Go and learn it.

– Hillel, *Talmud, Shabbath* 31a

Sikhism I am a stranger to no one; and no one is a stranger to me. Indeed, I am a friend to All.

– *Guru Granth Sahib*, pg. 1299

Taoism Regard your neighbour's gain as your own gain and your neighbour's loss as your own loss.

– Lao T'zu, *Ta'i Shang Kan Ying P'iea* 213-218

Unitarianism We affirm and promote respect for the interdependent web of all existence of which we are a part.
- Unitarian principle

Zoroastrianism Do not do to others whatever is injurious to yourself.
- *Shayast-na-Shayast* 13.29

Native Spirituality We are as much alive as we keep the earth alive.
- Chief Dan George

CONVERSATION IN AN OFFICE

This interview took place in Sister's office during normal working hours.

Is the concept of God the same across the board?

The Muslim concept of God is very close to the Catholic one: God as a person. As Christians, we have the spirit of God inside of us, but it is different from us; I am not God. The Buddhists deify their own prophet. The Hindus have their different gods and goddesses, and each of those deities is a personification of a particular attribute of God. The Hindus also believe that they are a sliver of God. That concept, in India, can lead to tremendous humility or tremendous arrogance. The arrogance is there, along with a need for power for those people lower down on the scale—interestingly, you don't find it so much in people with real power or in people who have accomplished a lot in their lives, as I've found them to be mostly humble people.

I'm thinking here of people like the railway clerk who tells you to get another signature on your piece of paper from the station principal, which you go ahead and do, and when you return, the clerk tells you that you need a further signature, and then another one, and so on.

Each thing is done one by one, never ever all together at the same time. It's a very common way for these people to exercise power.

Who are your heroes?

I don't have any favourite people at all, except for Jesus. I've never paid any attention to the rest of them.

I think I'm quite an egotistical person, because I don't look around and make heroes of people. You see, what do we mean by a "hero?" Someone you look up to, someone who's done something fantastic, someone you respect and admire. I don't want to say I don't respect or admire anybody. Actually, I think I respect and admire everybody. That's the simplest answer.

All the people we never really notice; lots of nuns who have borne the burden, who never opened their mouths to get any notice from anyone, just got on with their work. There are multitudes of them.

I see everybody the same way, everybody struggling in their own lives, heroic in their own way. Everyone's a hero.

Some people go mad over a particular film star or idol or a Nelson Mandela, a Mother Teresa, someone to whom they're devoted. If those people were to come into their lives, they would be thrilled.

I remember when I was in Rome for a conference, and we were to meet Pope John Paul—the one who was canonized recently—and we were brought into a very nice chapel. I was seated about halfway down, lots of nuns on either side of me, and when the Pope walked across to us, all of them got up and ran across to touch him. I couldn't do that. I thought, "Who is this man?" I could maybe do it for Jesus, but not for anybody else. I was just happy to be there and get his blessing, but that kind of worship leaves me absolutely cold.

How well do you know yourself?

Not very well at all. I don't need looking after, my body looks after itself. I've been a very healthy person all my life. I've never had to think about myself at all, so I don't look after myself.

No, on the other hand, I do. I do look after myself, otherwise I wouldn't be so healthy and surviving so well for so long with so much energy. So I do look after myself. Now, in this dreadfully hot weather, I've been going later for my dinner, then I go to my room, take off all my clothes and enjoy the coolness under the fan. That's looking after myself, isn't it?

I don't suffer from that politeness of leaving the last cake on the table for somebody else.

What's your connection to animals?

I simply love animals, all animals. I love every single form of life, but much more mammals, like horses, cows, kittens, cats, dogs. What else? Goats, also sheep. Actually though, sheep are not so attractive. Oh, and I also like lizards.

From when I was a small child I've always had pets. I had two cats, a big black one, and a black and white runt of the litter, and every day when I returned from school, she'd get up on a chair to catch hold of my dress and climb up on to my shoulder. I also had a dog. I still remember the day he came home inside of my father's coat, tiny thing called Spot.

I had very little family to play with at home because my brother and sister were four to five years older, and my parents didn't encourage us to bring other children home to play. When I was at home I was often alone, so these animals became my very close friends and playmates.

Do you think this planet can survive if men keep running it without the help of women?

No, it won't survive.

If women were in charge of our planet, would we have global warming and the other problems that assail us?

No, we would not have global warming as we have it. Women would certainly care for the planet better than men. Women can manage a home, look after half a dozen children—and a husband—and still do a full day's work in some kind of business, while most men can barely look after themselves!

I think women could take care of our planet just fine.

Which emotion do you use most on a daily basis?

(thinking for a long time) If someone poor comes into this office, someone really in great need, then love and care would be the dominant ones. But today, someone came to me who wouldn't listen at all, and although I have a lot of love for her, I snapped at her, and now I feel sorry.

I get impatient when I'm provoked. Provocation in the sense of someone being really stupid. I get irritated by the ineptness of what goes on in the government.

The Bengali habit of talking, talking, talking, talking about everything but doing nothing; they'll talk the hind leg off a donkey, but they won't do anything about it, and it drives me mad. The habit they have of interfering in everybody else's life. A young girl didn't want to get married, but all the old biddies in the neighbourhood were putting pressure on her, gossiping behind her back, and so I asked the girl, "Will they actually do anything to help you?" and of course the answer was no, so why pay attention to them? That's very irritating to me.

Do you ever feel stress?

Stress?

Let me tell you about stress.

Have you ever heard of "uptime"?

If you live in uptime, you are someone who is aware of what is happening all around you, but nowadays, most people are not living in uptime because they are so distracted by all the other things going on in their lives: Twitter, email, FB, ipods, ipads...

Uptime is living in the moment, intensely aware of all that you do, of everything around you. Creative thinking comes from being and living in uptime.

What happens when you're under a lot of stress?

"Reachback" and "Afterburn."

Your "reachback" is the amount of time you need to get yourself ready for the next event in your life, and your "afterburn" is the amount of time you need to get over the event that you've just finished. If these two things overlap, you become stressed and overloaded, a breakdown.

My reachback is about thirty minutes, and my afterburn is about 10 minutes, which is why I could always accomplish so many different things and not have a nervous breakdown. I didn't require much time at all to recover, but I know many people who require a fortnight or more to get ready for an upcoming event, and afterwards, they'll spend a long time cogitating and worrying about how it went.

That's fine if they're allowed the space to do this, but because things are becoming so much faster now, these people are not able to keep up because they are constantly getting ready for the next great thing.

Nobody is prepared to wait. There are tremendous pressures being exerted on people, particularly in business, to measure up in this highly competitive society we live in.

How do you come up with most of your ideas?

This might sound strange, but I have so much inside of me that has to come out. When I'm presented with some kind of problem, I'll get a solution to it without looking it up in a book. Most of my education papers in my folders came out of my head in response to some problem I faced.

"Creative thinking" to me means 2 things: When I look at something, I always wonder, how can I make something else out of it. And when I look at several things, I'm thinking, how can I put these together.

My father was the same. I remember he wanted to make a concrete roller for the garden, so he found a pipe and pushed a stick through it, filled it up with concrete and made his roller. We had things all over the house where he had made something out of something else that you thought couldn't really be done like that.

For me, everything comes from the problems that are in front of me. They stimulate me into thinking how I can solve them.

I'm a problem solver.

INTERLUDE

A FEW (CLEAN) IRISH LIMERICKS...

There once was a lady of Clyde
Who ate some green apples and died
The apples fermented inside the lamented
And made cider inside her inside

There once was a lady named Lynn
Who was so extraordinarily thin
When she sat in the shade to sip lemonade
She slipped through the straw and fell in

There was a young man named Mulhall
Who went to a fancy dress ball
He thought he would risk it
And go as a biscuit
But a dog ate him up in the hall

THE STUDENT COUNSELLOR (PART 1)

For me, spirituality is day-to-day living. You know, you could go and pray and spend a lot of time worshipping God, but if you don't see what needs to be done around you, that to me is not spirituality, that is running away from your daily life and avoiding responsibility as a human being.

To be very honest, I am not a churchgoer. I go only once a year, on Good Friday, if I have time. It's not that I'm doing huge things to change the world, it's just my way.

On Saturdays and Sundays, I do things that normally a person would not do in a church environment—I work for the elderly and the destitute. I have seen priests preaching in church about loving your neighbour, giving your food to anybody who's hungry, clothes to people who have none. But how does all this happen in real life, and how much of this is followed by the people who are listening to the preachers is a big question for me.

Outside the church, I see a person lying on the street without food, without adequate clothing, but nobody comes out of the church to give that person the food and clothes they have just heard about.

So, spirituality for me is living life the way God wants it, actually, really, not shutting yourself away from the realities of the world. If there is a need, meet the need. Act on it, just act on it, every minute, every day. Isn't that ultimately what God wants from us?

Giving peace, love, and a bit of affection to someone is a way you can bring peace to yourself. At the end of the day, if you go home and you have a bed to lie down on and can sleep well, it says a lot about your day, because you've been doing good things, you've been affecting people's lives—and they've affected you in some way or another.

That is why you can sleep peacefully. You may have the best bed in the world which has cost a lot of rupees, but you can't buy the sleep.

I don't have to be a nun or a priest to do that. Any lay person, anyone can be close to God without being spiritual at all in that sense—without being church spiritual.

You just know, you just know, when you do something for other people, the sheer joy in yourself tells you, yes, this is what God wants.

God always wants us to be happy in whatever shape or form or way you find it.

PART VI

Thoughts on India

Tolerance

Secularism and Festivals

Reincarnation

Education and Marriage

The Dowry System

Human Rights

Poverty and Culture

Brickfields

Change

India's Future

TOLERANCE

When Pope Benedict came to Kolkata, you should have seen the crowds that formed. Everyone came to me asking for a pass to his Mass on the Maidan, and of course, his blessing. On the morning he was to leave—they didn't reveal his route because they were terrified something might happen to him—I knew he was going to pass by our school gates, so we put a big banner up across the whole front of the school, "GOD BLESS YOU HOLY FATHER," and I sent a note to all our parents that we were expecting his Holiness to pass by at 7:30 the next morning.

When I arrived at 7 o'clock, there were so many people at our gate that I couldn't get in! They were waiting along the roadside, cheering and waving flags. The Popemobile came flying down the road, then slowed down when it got to us, and there he was, standing up, with no protection around him at all, as he turned and blessed us. Everyone shouted, "He blessed us, he blessed us!" and they felt as if it were the most important thing in the world, even though they were Hindus. That's why I feel very much a part of this country. They have tremendous faith here, and I tell everyone, "Christianity has no monopoly on virtue in India."

We Christians believe we have everything, but you know, we don't have everything at all! There is so much goodness in other religions, too, like you see here during the Puja festival, when the well-off families come with a big box of fireworks, and tell me they brought their children to join with the Rainbow children so they could enjoy the fireworks together. We want them to understand, they say, and to learn to share.

There is a real depth here. All the religious intolerance in India is politically motivated. There is no intolerance in this country except the stuff that is politically worked up. None. We all celebrate each other's feast days, and share in each other's offerings. In this school, I have three Muslims, three Hindus, and three Catholics on my staff, and we live together perfectly happily.

In south India, you'll find caste intolerance, but that's a different matter.

It's not religious, it's an internal matter amongst the Hindus themselves.

Basically, it's all about the higher castes not allowing the lower castes to come up in the world. In north India, people wouldn't tolerate that, they would look down on it.

The intolerance is entirely made up!

Look at the Middle East. Part of the whole problem with terrorism is that these places have a lot of young, adolescent boys who have been brainwashed by the things that are broadcast in Urdu and Arabic, presented in such a way as to incite anger.

Part of it is historical injustice, and people being oppressed for years, and part of it is the indoctrination of the young. This indoctrination is, however, based on some facts, areas where people have been very deprived. And not necessarily deprived by the people who have been accused of depriving them, but by much wider powers outside.

You'd have to work a lot with these young men to slowly help them to understand the propaganda. You'd have to go to the madrassas, where these seeds of hate are being sown, and unfortunately in India, you would have to go into some of the Hindu schools where political elements are doing likewise.

But not all schools are like this. I have had wonderful education courses with headmasters of madrassa schools where they were genuinely concerned about the deterioration of values they find in their young and the difficulties in controlling their teenage boys.

We need a common school system to be put in place, which everyone attends, to be filled with teachers who listen, who can talk to each other, and who are filled with love themselves.

SECULARISM AND FESTIVALS

Towards the end of each year, we have many festivals in India. October is Puja, celebrating all the Hindu Gods, where the first five days are for everybody, followed by smaller events of one or two days spread over the whole month. Shortly after Puja is the Sikh festival Guru Nanak Day in November; and Eid, the Muslim festival is usually somewhere in between those two because it's a movable feast. Christmas comes last.

If you go into a junior school in India at this time, you'll see all the Gods and Goddesses—the whole Hindu pantheon with all the relevant information alongside the names—together with all the stuff about Guru Nanak, Eid, and Christmas, with pictures of Jesus and the crib. All of them are celebrated by every child, and they all get to eat every festival's sweets and cakes. I think this is the true spirit of secularism, that all religions are equal, that we celebrate and honour each other's religion. We don't fight over them.

Each child is very aware of who they are individually, and they also know that they are Hindus, Muslims, Sikhs, Buddhists, Christians and that we all pray to a common god.

In India, faith plays a tremendous part in people's lives.

India really believes.

It has a lot it could teach other countries in terms of tolerance. We are a nation of believers, we are not a nation of idolaters. I feel, sometimes, when people come here from the outside, they have this preconceived notion, but the Hindus no more worship idols than we in the West worship statues.

The Gods and Goddesses of the Puja are made of mud and straw, and when finished, are all brought together and installed in large pandals—bamboo frames over which a cheap but fine material is stretched—and bright lights are shone through the front of it, so that as they proceed down the street, people can see a variety of lit-up scenes: a painted castle, or a cathedral, or Mother Teresa in a church.

Inside of these pandal frames sits the pantheon of mud and straw Puja Gods and Goddesses, who have been prayed over by the priests, and the spirit of God has been allowed to enter them. When people look at these clay images, they believe—just as we do when we look at the Blessed Sacrament—that God's spirit is inhabiting the Puja Pandals. It's all quite beautiful. When the Puja is over, the priests pray to allow God's spirit to leave them, after which the poor are given all the finery from the images, and the clay Gods are all carried away to the Ganges and returned to the river.

REINCARNATION

You only get one chance in life. There is no reincarnation.

I don't believe in it, and I don't believe anyone else in India believes in it, either. If they did, they would treat animals much better than they do. They are very cruel to animals here, very cruel, unbelievably cruel.

How can people in India believe in reincarnation and at the same time treat animals so terribly? If they really believed in it, they wouldn't beat their dog so much, because they could in fact be beating their reincarnated grandmother! It's a concept for me that doesn't hold true in reality.

Even though I love cats, I won't come back as one. We've been given one chance here on earth to do our best and beyond that, we go back to God. Our souls float about in the ether somewhere, but I believe they return to enjoy face to face conversations with Jesus and God, and we meet all our other friends there.

A friend of mine calls heaven, "our cloud of witnesses."

In the New Testament, Jesus never talked about coming back, it was just one chance, and that was it, but he added that if you said sorry at the last minute on your deathbed—even if you had done dreadful things in your life—all was forgiven. Only those who die turned away from God go to hell, if there is indeed a hell. I am not sure if there is one. Jesus called it an eternal fire, and personally, I'm not prepared to risk that.

I think hell is having lost your chance forever. You are going to have to live—wherever that might be—separated from your body with nothing around you at all to cushion you from the reality of that. There is always a way back for us humans while we're alive, but once we're separated from our bodies, there isn't.

I don't think we can get back into some other body and relive it all over again.

EDUCATION AND MARRIAGE

In our early years, our patterns are laid down, especially from our parents, and that's why so many girls with drunken fathers marry drunken husbands. They've seen it so they know it, and the cycle has been programmed into them before the age of five that this is the kind of man they should marry. To break out of that they need education, to be helped and counselled. And yet we have sixteen-year-old girls we have educated and struggled with, who walk out with the first boy who comes along, and he'll be exactly like the kind of father who deserted their mother.

We have to get them past this point, and it is not always easy. It's hard to break the patterns; you have to be very conscious of them and help the girls to become conscious of what is happening inside them. To marry young is the only way to be safe, so their parents often believe. They don't want the responsibility of an eighteen-year-old living in those little hutments, because they don't know what'll happen to them in the night.

Whereas the children who come here, the Rainbows, they have a better chance, because they're going to school and getting a good education. The parents can think we don't have to marry her off, as she's safe in school. When they leave here, the girls go into an integration flat, and when they're ready and can get a decent job and can pay for their keep, they move into a hostel. So they never have to go back and live in the hutments.

But many parents still keep thinking of finding a "suitable boy." Even if their daughter is doing well in school, they will pull her out because for them getting a good husband is the highest priority. Now, for these girls who live on the street, to find a boy who has a decent, regular, permanent job, who's off the street, living in a small dwelling, and who doesn't drink, smoke or take drugs is a good match. So, as soon as they find one, they marry fast before someone else gets him, and that's why they get married so young. This is the difference between the poverty culture of the very poor and the lower middle class into which some of them move, after they make a "good" marriage.

In the poverty culture there is no future. To be able to see far enough ahead to when the girl will finish school and get a good job is in many cases impossible. However, our experience has been that many of these very girls who were pulled out of school into early marriages are now able to see the value of education for their own children. They are coming back now, saying we came too late to benefit fully, but we see the importance of education now and we want our children here.

THE DOWRY SYSTEM

One of the reasons why families traditionally didn't celebrate the birth of a daughter as much as a son is because the dowry immediately became a financial liability. And the girls themselves didn't want to marry into a family that expected a dowry, because if it were thought to be insufficient, the girl could be tortured by the mother-in-law, and in some cases, subjected to burning.

When we say "burning," what happens?

The in-laws are quite capable of locking the girl in a room, dowsing her in kerosene, setting her alight, and leaving her there to die.

We're talking about "good families" here, families of "good social standing" who are financially affluent, with a reputation to lose, where the neighbours tell you after the event they heard the screaming and the shouting.

In West Bengal now, if there is a death in the family due to burning, the police will immediately arrest the father, mother and the husband, and they have to prove they're innocent, rather than the other way around. Because of this, deaths of young married women have greatly decreased here.

There is also a greater respect for daughters nowadays, because they can be educated and become a family breadwinner. I can't produce any scientific evidence, but I think there has been a change in attitudes, and daughters are more cherished now than they were before. The columns in the local newspapers are full of words like, "convent-educated," "degrees," "training" of some sort, and these qualifications have become a form of compensation for the dowry, they add to the term "well-married."

The original reason for a dowry was that if the marriage didn't work out, if the girl was turned out by the groom's family, the dowry acted as a form of protection, it supported her. But in fact, that turned out to be untrue, because the groom's family came to see it as additional income.

Educated girls see the dowry as insulting; to pay to have your daughter taken away by a boy! Loreto girls ask, "Why don't the boys have to pay to get a wife?" They do not agree at all that their families have to pay the boy's family to take her off their hands. I think, if left to themselves, the young of today would dispense with the system altogether, but the problem has traditionally been the mother-in-law, who doesn't want to give up the money, nor the virtual "slave" that marries into her family to obey her every whim.

And nowadays, with affluence steadily increasing in India, the parents of the girls themselves want to keep the dowry system because they can show off their newfound wealth and prestige. The mothers now try to outdo each other, as to how much of a dowry they can afford to pay. The whole one-upmanship of it all, it's just basic egotism, which we need to try and grow out of.

Prestige in India is a very big thing. If someone insults you, your honour is destroyed. My reaction to this is that it's not your honour that goes, it's theirs. They've insulted you, and in doing that, they let themselves down. But people here don't see it that way.

If I was still young (and not a nun!), I too, would refuse a dowry.

When I first came to India fifty years ago, the dowry system was much more prevalent, in fact, the whole basis of family life was stronger, because the majority of families were still joint families. The boys got married and brought their wives home, where they all resided together under one roof. Everyone met at mealtimes and for certain important family meetings, making everything that much more cohesive. The grandparents had a much greater control over the grandchildren, as well as over their sons and daughters, whereas, nowadays, there's been a huge shift to nuclear families, where the young couple lives somewhere else altogether. The grandchildren are growing up in a very different milieu, and the grandparents have very little say in it.

Another difference is the amount of money a young person had. When they began to work, their starting salaries were so small they had no choice but to continue living with their families; they couldn't move out. College was not so common as it is now. Mobility again has brought huge changes to this, broken down huge barriers.

The dowry is still with us, but it's more like a dinosaur. It's also forbidden by law. There's also a law, a ceiling, for how much can be spent at a wedding, but it's not enforced.

There is now litigation that controls the amount of money you can give in a dowry, there is increasing anger and strong reactions to "bride-burning" in the countryside, and girls are no longer being married off without them having seen the man first. Girls are beginning to have a choice.

One of my teachers told me her story. When she was seventeen years old, her mother told her to pack her bags and put on her best sari, because the girl's sister in Delhi had found her a nice, young boy. She told her mother she didn't want to get married, she wasn't ready, but her mother reminded her that her sister would suffer at the hands of her in-laws in Delhi if she didn't go and meet the boy. So, she packed her bags full of jeans and t-shirts and went to Delhi where she and the nice boy were put in a separate room to talk to each other, and where she frightened the wits out of him by firing all kinds of questions at him. The next day, the boy's mother told her sister that she was much too smart for her son and withdrew their offer. She was sent back home in disgrace, but secretly thrilled, because she was already involved with another boy at home. She subsequently got married to him and has been happily married for thirty years.

HUMAN RIGHTS

Everyone is born equal, but if you are born into a rich family, you are more protected than if you are poor. The poor don't have the same access as the rich do to lawyers, judges, police commissioners and the like, and therefore their rights are often in jeopardy.

An accountant for our school, a nice young man, was taken by the police at 1:00 am from his mother's house, and arrested for a crime committed two days earlier. Afterwards, he was brought before the court and charged with having seven bullets in his pocket.

But a dreadful mistake had been made, because the same young man had actually been in jail two days earlier, charged with another crime that he hadn't committed. So, I went to see the Assistant Commissioner, then the Deputy Commissioner, then finally I got to see the Man-in-Charge, and told him it was a case of mistaken identity because the young man's mother had a police receipt from when he had been arrested previously, when the so-called crime occurred.

The Commissioner said to me, "These men have to be kept off the streets. We need to keep them locked up, because unless we have a good case against them, the judge won't put them in jail for us."

Outraged, I told him that the young man was an accountant for our school and a respectable citizen. "Does this mean, sir, you might pick me up off the street in the middle of the night, too?" I asked him.

"No, no, of course not, we'd never do that kind of thing to someone like you, Sister," he assured me.

Eventually I got our accountant out, but for the next two months, he insisted on sleeping at school, so terrified was he of going out. By the way, the "seven bullets" was simply a fabrication to make the case more sensational.

Two Chinese brothers were sitting on the steps of their parents' food shop in Kolkata on a holiday, when they were picked up by the police, put in jail, and told if they signed some papers they would be let go. The idiots didn't read the papers and signed, after which the police accused them of being drug dealers. At this point, the parents came to me asking what could be done but it was too late; they'd already signed. Never ever sign anything!

As the police have told me many times, it's only ever going to happen to the little people, not the ones with clout.

I had a car that I sold to a teacher, who lent it to her son to drive up to Darjeeling with two friends. On the way, they were stopped by the police, and the other two boys ran away. The son was taken into custody, signed a paper, and was charged with smuggling. The car was impounded for six months. Much, much later, I was able to get the car back and get the son out.

A man who was employed as a Pest Control Officer went into a building to do a job when suddenly the building caught fire. He was accused by a Civil Service Officer of starting the fire and being a terrorist. The accuser wouldn't back down and admit he was wrong. In the end, the accused was only released because his boss stood up for him.

There are hundreds of cases like this of real people, little people, in horrible situations where their human rights have been violated, and who knows how many hundreds more that we never even hear about.

POVERTY AND CULTURE

What kind of poverty? The kind that leaves you with no resources, no security, no future. You live in the present because experience has shown you that tomorrow may never come, so whatever you earn today, you spend, and hope that tomorrow may be better and if it is not, then you keep your head down and survive as long as you can. Whatever comes to hand, make use of it, whether it's an old tire to keep the bits of straw from blowing off your roof or something off the garbage dump that you can recycle.

Poverty.

There is nowhere in the West that can compare to here. If you go anywhere in Ireland today, you'll not see anyone living in the kinds of shacks you'll find at Eastern Bypass. They have no future. No identity. No voice. No address.

Because it's a non-recognized slum, they have no eligibility to vote, no ration card, so no capacity to be able to buy cheaper food.

Many of these services are already set up for the poor, but not for people on the level I'm talking about. They are at the very bottom of the pile, and there is no access for them whatsoever.

A minimum of 150-250 million of the Indian population live like this, according to the World Bank. Millions upon millions of people. It's very difficult to check these kinds of statistics for many reasons, one of them being that the government itself tries to skew them into making India appear better than it really is.

When we started the Rainbow Homes, a police officer told us the first thing to do was to get every single child registered so they could get their papers. The West Bengal Corporation agreed to register every child we had for 50 paisa (1 cent), so at the very least the children would have papers. Without them, they would be lost, they wouldn't exist.

This is what happens to many of the itinerant workers at the brickfields who return home for several months at the beginning of the monsoons in June. During that time, if they can get themselves registered in their hometown, they can be eligible for various services. Otherwise, they get nothing and are totally at the mercy of the brickfield owners, when they return to Kolkata in November.

But as terrible as the poverty is, it's a poverty of material things, not cultural. No matter how poor or weak the children, if you play some Indian music, watch as their hands and bodies move perfectly. Give them a bit of chalk and watch the beautiful designs they draw without any real effort. They have a culture that goes back thousands of years to when the rest of us were living in caves.

The East was the cradle of civilization, so when we're dealing with these children, why should we feel we've got to teach them anything, in terms of Western culture? Why can't we just leave them alone and be happy with that?

I only have one dream for all the children of India. Give them enough food so they're not brain-damaged before the age of five, give them good quality education, which challenges them to think and seek out solutions to their own problems, and leave them to make their own way to build their own country. I have seen this happening again and again. Educate them to be responsible for their decisions and the values they live by. You don't do this by constantly watching them, but by leaving them free. They need our trust, if they are to grow and be empowered.

BRICKFIELDS

Dust in your hair, in your eyebrows, in your mouth, in every mouthful of food, in every breath ...And heat. Once March comes, each day is that little bit hotter, until by June it becomes unbearable but has to be lived through until the welcome grey clouds gather heavy with rain. But by then everyone has to leave, as you can't make bricks in the rain...

Thousands of families migrate each year from Bihar, Chhattisgarh and over the border into West Bengal bringing their children with them, camping out in atrocious conditions, working from dawn to dusk.

Making bricks.

It takes the whole family the whole day to make a thousand bricks, for which they get paid 200 rupees. This requires the combined efforts of all family members, so there is no time for the children to get on a bus and go to school, even if a school were available.

That is why we negotiated with the brickfield owners to allow us to open schools inside the brickyards so the children can go to school and at the same time help their parents. The classrooms consist of a circle of bricks with a child seated on each one. One little boy's bottom is so small that he can sit on a tiny brick!

When we started the Loreto "Brickfields Project" a few years ago, we had no guarantee that the families would be returning to the same brickfield every fall, as they are employed by contractors, but many have been making great efforts to come back to the same place in order to continue their children's schooling.

Our next effort now is to negotiate with the Education Department to make some arrangement whereby they can be admitted to schools in their home states when they are there from June to November.

If this is successful, we will see yet another group of marginalized children enabled to take their rightful place in society.

CHANGE

Many people may think that India hasn't changed that much, but in the last fifty years that I've been here I can definitely say that it has changed a lot. First of all, there's been a huge increase in mobility, a huge increase in communications.

Take the example of the domestic staff in Loreto Sealdah, where we had four men from Orissa state (now Odisha), several hundred miles to the south. In the old days, they would go home once a year for their holidays, and that was it. Otherwise, they never saw their families. Nowadays, these same men can talk to their families any time they like on their mobile telephones, as practically everybody has one. Secondly, the opportunities for poorer people have greatly increased. A child educated by us and coming from the lowest slum can now go to the very top of the corporate sector, and nobody would oppose her. A low-caste Dalit, Narayanan, an untouchable, became President of India not so long ago.

The prejudices from before have been greatly reduced, although the prejudice can remain if the person hasn't been educated. But if they've received a good education and can carry themselves well, they do have a chance.

Earlier, the very deep-rooted Hindu caste system made equality impossible. But now, the caste system has, to a large extent, broken down in many parts of the country, but not all. Here in West Bengal, because it was influenced by the British, a great deal of Christianization has happened, and the big Hindu revivals and the Communist Party have also brought about great change.

India has seen huge growth in the number of cities, the number of flyovers in those cities, metro systems. Kolkata is now building an overland metro to the south of the city.

Visually, India has changed, too.

In 1956, there were no high-rise buildings when we first arrived in Kolkata, with thirty trunks full of odd parcels and out-of-date Irish newspapers given by nuns in Ireland to their counterparts in India, many of whom thought they would never see each other again. Many of the ones who arrived in the 1920s and '30s didn't get back to Ireland until the 1950s. I had told my parents that I'd be able to make it home once, but I had no idea when that might be. I personally know of nuns in Australia who never got home at all.

In those days, it took three weeks by ship from Ireland to India by way of South Africa; letters took the same amount of time. It sounds unbelievable to me now, but that's the way it was. Remember also, that when I arrived, it was only a few years after India had got its independence from the British, so we couldn't buy biscuits or chocolate, because Nehru, India's Prime Minister, had stopped all imports and was only dealing in local goods, which is why the local industries are so strong to this day. Indian biscuits and chocolate are the equal of anywhere in the world!

Many of the backstreets, however, in Kolkata have not changed at all, except that now, they'd have access to piped water, electricity, and in some places, you might get a TV, but that would be the limit.

I don't think, though, that people are happier.

Fifty years ago, there was none of the culture of rich people showing off. You didn't have the range of materials available that can be bought today. If you were poor, you weren't so conscious of the people who had things, because the level that people mixed at was less, and you didn't really know what was going on. Even the rich families were lower key; they didn't show off their riches, whereas the nouveau riche of today want to show off their brand names, and the result of all this is a great deal of envy.

People buy things so that others will think well of them; status has become important. The original families of the Rajas, the Maharajas, seemed to carry their riches more lightly because they knew they had it. I've heard junior school students in this city saying, "I only wear this brand name or that brand name." Something is wrong when children so young say it.

Students have changed a lot as well. They've become more sophisticated, much more aware of the issues than before. The levels of communication, iPods, iPads—they're all very well up on computers.

The simplicity from before has gone out of them, they're now dressing up, more conscious of clothes. The choices are huge. Girls are much freer than before, so parents worry more. You see boys and girls walking in the street holding hands—you would never ever ever have seen that fifty years ago, it would have been totally unacceptable! Girls have become ever more revealing, it seems, because before they were always so well covered up; girls usually wore a sari, never a pair of jeans or a tight skirt.

The "mall culture" is another change, these great big malls all over the place, and I suspect, with the high prices they charge, many families go there on the weekends to simply get out of the heat, sit in the beautiful air-conditioning and enjoy the coolness. I suppose people must be buying something, otherwise the shops couldn't continue, but when I see belts advertised for 1000 rupees (10 GBP) and bags for 5000 rupees (50 GBP)...!

I was in a village a while ago where I heard the sound of all these machines. When I peered into a hot, darkened room, I saw it was full of men on pedal sewing machines, busy stitching leather jackets with American insignia all over them. When I asked them what they were doing, they replied, "We'll sell the jackets in Chowringhee (a main street in Kolkata) as smuggled goods, so people think they're getting a bargain from America!"

INDIA'S FUTURE

India is one of the most technologically, economically advanced nations of the world. And if it can adequately provide for 70 percent of its population below the poverty line, I see a bright future for India.

There are a lot of parallels between this country as it is now and Irish and European societies as they were at the end of the nineteenth century. When I was growing up in rural Ireland, I remember everyone as being poor, very poor. Most families in Ireland wouldn't have had a car. People used horses and traps to get around. In the Victorian era, the music and dance masters came in to teach the daughters of the well-off families, and the same thing is happening here now. The girls then didn't go out without a chaperone, which is true here now. It's only recently that India has begun to emerge out of that Victorian way of living...

If India is able to handle the burden of still having a huge amount of its people below the poverty line, I see it as being a leader in the future.

India is already a leader for values. It is the only country in Southeast Asia that's never had a military coup. We've always had elections. Yes, there's been fighting and violence, but nothing has ever prevented the lawfully, legally elected party from taking power. And there has never been any revenge on the outgoing party, as has happened so often in other Asian and African countries. India has preserved the value for human life, value for just and properly passed laws. The parliamentary system has remained, because Hinduism is a very tolerant and wise religion with a very long history.

Unfortunately, these days, there is a certain veneer coming from leaders, a crowd who see money as being very important. I always find it interesting to watch these wealthy people fighting to get their children into our schools! Why is that? Because of the value systems, and however rich and corrupt some of them might be, they can still discern these inherent values and want them for their children!

Another interesting point about all of this is that there is corruption, a lot of it, but it is out in the open, not hidden. The media, on the whole, are fair and just. There's a lawfully elected judiciary, which has so far proved largely incorruptible, and I think that often saves the country, because when things become law, the judges are good.

A problem recently has been that all the political parties have been shouting "India is shining," "It's the millionaire of the world," and this has affected people's readiness to give money to the poor here. Many organizations have been affected, because people only see the super rich and their kind of people, and the assets of politicians seeking power. It's obscene to think that every elected member of Parliament is given 1 crore (100,000 GBP) to spend on his constituency, which they do not spend on their villages. Many of these same people have been in prison or charged with bribery and scams and various corrupt practices, taking beyond what's their due.

The solution is very simple: if I were elected and had all that money, I would divide my constituency up into small squares, like a chessboard, and I would complete a square each year where everyone got their health centre, a well for clean drinking water, a school of sufficient size with properly trained teachers who were regularly checked to see whether they were doing a good job. The country could be transformed in no time at all!

Things are happening: RTE (Right to Education, 2009) and RTI (Right to Information, 2005) have both been passed. RTW (Right to

Work, 2005) was also passed, guaranteeing that everybody gets a minimum of 100 days of work a year. Every state was given money for this, but many states who weren't part of the main party either gave the money back or took it for themselves.

Some things, it seems, take a long time to change.

INTERLUDE

THE LORETO "BRICKFIELDS PROJECT" MANAGER

The children here are very difficult to mainstream, as they can't spend a full school term or a year anywhere. Some of them may only have six months here; they won't be coming back, as these people roam all over India—next year they might be making bricks in Punjab—so in the short time they spend in our schools we try to make that experience as happy as possible.

Their world is very limited, but we thought if we can expand their horizons, then maybe they'll challenge their reason for being here in the brickfields, and in the future, possibly break out of this cycle.

We're trying to develop their minds.

Usually, I work in fields where the government doesn't, I do things that society says can't be done. People say it's not possible to open schools for migrant populations. So I say, okay, if these people are travelling to different places every six months, then our school will follow them. Our intention here is to bring the school to them. I like the idea that the school follows the children, not the other way around.

When I look around here, it works, definitely. I see children learning in a broader way. Many of them have never learned the alphabet, but they do know words and sentences, so sometimes, we teach the sentences first then go back to the letter or character.

They're also learning about their culture, learning about their country and also basic things about themselves. I think that's important. What we try to achieve is to open their perspectives, to challenge their lives.

I cannot conduct a revolution for them. If they want to break out of the brickfields, they have to find a way to break the bricks. I don't believe you can fight for others. How can I change any of this? If you feel that your present status is not right, only you can start the change, and once you start that, I can help you.

You can't do a revolution for the people; many have tried and failed. It took us millions of years to get from monkeys to human beings, but we still kill, still bomb other people's countries, still invent toys of war, so we're still not human beings.

I just try to inspire them, that's all, light the first match, make a spark. I can't assume that I know everything. I always start from the point of view that I have something to learn, and in the process, I share what I know with them.

I always learn, like my ideas about poverty completely changed when I started working inside the brickfields, because I never imagined that people could be this poor. What I think of as the basic minimum standard of living is heaven for them; things about which I complain, they completely accept. My daughter complains if I don't take her to McDonald's once a month, but these children don't even have toys. Many of them don't even have proper clothes.

They work for less than $3 a day—that's a unit of five people, not one, so they're actually working for less than $1 a day—and that's temporary work for six to eight months only. After that's done, nothing.

For a country like ours there are no quick solutions; there's no quick fix for us, no.

How can you fix their lives?

There are approximately 4000 brickfields in West Bengal, each one with about 30-40 families living there. Is that instantly fixable?

There are migrant fishermen's groups like this, too, who follow the fish; people who work on local farms who also roam all over India. There is a huge, internal migrant population which does all the odd jobs to make the lives of people like us easier.

Whenever I go back and play with my child, I feel very sad. The very basic minimum for my child will never ever be the same for the children I work for. The economic status would be impossible for them; even my salary they couldn't possibly hope to earn in a lifetime.

Maybe I'll get in trouble for saying this, but for me, the brickfields are nothing more than slavery: contemporary slavery. There's no barbed wire, no security guards, but they are slaves.

The walls here are social walls they can't break. These children cannot compete with my child in any way, in any exams, in any interview, to get a job. Having only one choice is not a choice, and they have no choice but to work here. Yes, we can say, they willingly work here, they've negotiated a wage, but they've zero negotiating power compared to the brickfields owner. If they don't work, other people will.

No rights. No fixed working hours. No fixed salary.

My only dream for them is that their children will not work in the brickfields, but I don't see any easy solution for them. I don't see this young girl standing next to me working in an office in a big city. I don't see it, I don't see it, but I'll be very happy to be proved wrong.

I worry about them, I even cry that I can't do anything; all I'm doing is making reports and other things, that's all. Their lives are not going to change quickly, and it makes me sad and depressed sometimes, yes. I think I should leave and go and work in a glass box in the city, in a secure job where all the people are like me, but I can't.

I remind myself that these bricks they are making are used to build my house.

A MESSAGE FROM THE ALUMNI

Village work...
is not walking long distances in the heat—
it is walking into people's hearts.

Village work...
is not long hours away from home—
it is some time spent in the reality of life.

Village work...
is not about the young working for the younger—
it is about dreaming of a brighter India.

Village work...
is not about a bus full of girls in uniform—
it is about several kids who eagerly await their arrival.

Village work...
is not about completing the lesson plan in two hours—
it is about the number of hearts touched in that period of time.

Village work...
is not about earning accolades—
it is about bringing forth a realization.

PART VII

Thoughts on Sexuality

Sex and Sexuality

The Fantastic Fantasy

Educating Boys

Strong Women

Sex in Marriage

Abuse

SEX AND SEXUALITY

Some years back, I was asked to prepare a course for young couples contemplating marriage. One of the topics covered was Sex and Sexuality, and I was asked what was the difference between them.

Sex is what we have in common with all plants and animals. the ability to reproduce our own kind.

Sexuality is sex linked into your own personality, how we relate to each other as men or as women.

We have a completely different psychology.

Here's an example. For the girl, the boy is the only person she wants, she is the desire to be desired, and she wants him to be everything for her. She looks at every boy for the possibility that he will like her, which is why, when girls go to parties, they take a lot of trouble with the way they dress. Boys don't do this because they don't have to impress so much, they can just take.

The man goes first for the pleasure of the sexual relationship. She goes for something much deeper. That's why women get more hurt in casual relationships, especially these days, because they give of themselves totally, but the man doesn't.

Here's another example. A couple is coming home from a party, and he says to her, "Didn't Mrs So-and-so look nice in that sari?" and she says, "What were you looking at her for? Who am I? Am I nothing in your life?" And his thinking is, "What did I say? I only said such a little thing..."

He doesn't realize he has touched a vital nerve in his wife, which is that he is not supposed to have anybody else in his life except her. Men find this difficult to understand. "He never tells me he loves me," women complain. She needs to be told every other day that he loves her. He thinks he doesn't need to do that, he told her last week, last month, a year ago, what more does she want?

A lot of fights begin this way, and I help couples with little things like this.

Of course, I've never been married myself, but I had the first seventeen years of my life within my family. I have no regrets I never got married, but I do have observations to make, oh yes! Look what I escaped: crying babies, walking the floor in the middle of the night, teething.

Instead, I have, at Loreto, thousands of children...

I have no husband but Jesus. A marriage, but not a human one. For me, He's a little higher up the list. A higher husband, but what a wonderful person to know and love.

THE FANTASTIC FANTASY

I talk to my Class 6 ten- and eleven-year-olds about sex and sexuality, because many of them live up on the roofs of high-rise buildings, playing and experimenting with other boys and girls, or watching older boys and girls together. I do the work as a 'fantasy exercise.'

I say to them: "Close your eyes, and go right down into your toes. Feel them, and your muscles, flex them, make them strong." And slowly, like this, I work up through the whole of their body, right out through the top of their head. Then I say, "Now, open your eyes, look at the palm of your hand. That's God's imprint on you. Nobody in the whole world has ever had a palm and a set of fingerprints like you, and out of all the millions and millions who have been created throughout time, no two fingerprints are alike. You are unique. There is no one else in the world like you. Simply give praise to God for who you are. Look at yourself very carefully. Your skin, feel how it grows, how it gets bigger if you put on weight, and gets less if you get thinner. If you cut it, it heals itself. How beautiful it is, so how beautiful God must be to have created us..."

If you've ever seen a baby squirrel inside its mother's womb, they're all folded up, like little parcels, and all their nails on their fingers are perfect, and you realize what a fantastic brain it must be to have brought all this beauty to life.

Then I ask them all, "How did you begin? How did all this begin? How were you created? Your mummy and daddy were very close together and loving each other very much, and the sperm came from your daddy, and you became a being when that sperm went into an egg belonging to your mummy. It was all so tiny. Think about how small you were, and yet, God breathed life into you. Inside your mother, you grew and grew, and when the time was right, out you came, and here you are now. Stop and think, stop and think about that."

Then I ask them, "When you have something very beautiful, do you throw it into the gutter for the pigs, or do you keep it carefully inside of yourself and care for it? Sex is the capacity to make a new human being out of your very own body. You don't throw it away. You wait until the right time, look after it and bring it up well."

You have to be careful how much detail you give them until the age of eleven or twelve, as it can be frightening, but that's it in a nutshell.

EDUCATING BOYS

Men are the same all over the world. They have needs that we women do not always have. When a boy looks at a girl, to fulfil his lust, he sees her shape and thinks of his pleasure; the girl looks at the boy because she wants affection and love.

We give the Loreto girls proper instruction about sex and sexuality, but I'm sure the boys don't get any instruction at all in schools. No training on how to respect women, nothing. Unfortunately in India, males are not taught respect by their mothers because they are treated as little gods. In Hindu society, they are worshipped.

The whole society is phallic, the idea of fertility where the man is the god and the women is subservient. The fact that she produces a child goes unnoticed.

When a male is put into a situation where he is tempted, and his hormones are working overtime seeing this object of pleasure before him, he goes for it. He doesn't think, because he has never been asked from childhood to deny himself. He has always been given everything; if he wants a glass of water he'll tell his sister to go and fetch it for him.

In the West, boys aren't brought up to think of themselves as Gods. They're expected to help out in the house like everyone else. Nobody is going to mollycoddle them so they can sit around and let the women do all the work. The women won't take it. Western girls are brought up to be more equal, so if someone comes at them and they don't want it, they can fight. Many girls in India simply wouldn't know what to do and panic.

I am pledged to girl's education, but if I were in charge of boys, I would spend some time in getting them to reflect on what their relationship to women should be and the kind of respect that should be shown to them.

I would also prepare men for life, for community, not competition. Many people see that as a weakness, but you can still win without becoming obsessed about it. Educate them that winning is not necessarily always the best for them. Men are going to fail at some point in life, and they have to be able to accept that, be able to deal with that.

Let them have a protective feeling towards women, especially towards their wives, and a sense of caring towards society. I'm always quite happy that boys wrestle and punch each other up and do a bit of rough-housing. I did all of that, too, when I was young.

Strangely, I probably have more friends among men than women. These days, I find myself on so many committees where I'm the only female there.

But I admit I quite enjoy bossing all the men around.

STRONG WOMEN

Men and women should be equal, but different. Women provide the egg, and men provide the sperm, so both are equal and necessary, and yet in every modern society, women have got it worse.

As a child in India, the girl is under her father, and as she gets older she's under her brother, and when she gets married she's under her husband, and when he dies she's under her sons, so she is never an independent person! If she wants equality, she has to fight for it.

The sad irony of it is, in my opinion, women are much stronger than men! A man just has to get sick, to see how strong he really is. That's why women bear children, not men. It would be too painful for them, they'd never make it! Women's lives are fraught with suffering, not only physical, but mental, emotional.

If there's a picnic and not everyone can go, guess who will stay at home: the mother. It won't be anyone else.

And what about those beautiful, well educated girls in places like the Middle East, where the doors are suddenly closed on them after their studies. They have to return to their families and endure whatever comes their way. Many of them are married off to a man they don't want. They see their children, whom they've given everything they have to, grow up and move away. That takes a lot of inner strength.

Another thing women have to deal with—women all over the world, rich or poor—is domestic violence. Respect a woman who can hold her own with dignity, who doesn't wilt in a verbal argument with a man. And think of all those who are mauled by drunken husbands but suffer through that silently for the sake of their children; they can't walk out. So much strength.

This is all very different to the image of muscular, Amazonian-type women who kickbox, do wrestling and other extreme physical sports. That's all fine if they want that.

But feminine women are equally as strong. The women in Kolkata are still feminine—being manly is not their way of being equal to a man.

And just like them, I want to be as I am.

A woman.

And a very strong one at that!

SEX IN MARRIAGE

We are born either male or female. That obvious fact is probably the most important determinant in our lives. Before we leave the hospital nursery we are designated pink or blue. From then on, everything we do—our tastes, attitudes, education, occupation, emotional reactions, and our images of self, others, and the world—is influenced, even determined, by our sexual identity.

We begin learning our sexual attitudes at a very young age, even before we are freed from the crib. We learn them from parents, friends, schools, church, and the mass media. They teach us in a variety of ways, by direction and indirection, by words, actions, and silence.

Our parents teach it in their communication towards each other, by their reactions to nudity and childhood sexual exploration, by what they don't say about sex as well as what they do say.

Unfortunately, our society has a long and sad history of negative attitudes towards sex and of outright anti-sexualism. And if our parents have less than truly positive attitudes themselves, they can't successfully teach positive attitudes either.

Women's and men's magazines present a picture of marriage and sexuality which is often immature, at times distorted. And with so much anti-sexualism and cynicism present in our society, one would have to have both a very positive orientation and a great deal of self-assurance to withstand its influence.

The sickness is all around us.

When was the last time you read a love story about a husband and wife? Or saw a movie in which sexual love was not illicit?

Irrational sexual attitudes affect every dimension of the marital relationship. But with so many of these unhealthy attitudes accepted by our culture as "normal," we may not recognize them as irrational and may hence fail to see the pernicious effect they are having on marriage.

It's common for some to speak of "having sex" rather than "making love." They will say it doesn't necessarily represent anything as far as their attitudes are concerned. But it does. "Having sex" de-personalizes it and places it on the level of strict satisfaction of a physical appetite, no different from eating when hungry or drinking when thirsty.

Even if you call it "making love," do you see it as the making of love, as a true commitment, a mutual giving of self? Or is it little more than copulating or mutual masturbating?

We strongly disagree with those who make marital bliss dependent solely on the acquisition of sexual athletic skills and a vivid imagination. Not only are they simplistic in approach, they reduce marriage to a romp in bed, and humans to mating animals.

Is coitus the "high point" of your love-making, a love-making which goes on throughout the day in countless ways of affection and concern, or is it merely a periodic response to genital tension?

One of the saddest examples of the latter is seen in the couple who seemingly declare an armistice in their fighting long enough to engage in sexual relations and then resume the hostilities.

If you find no emotional and spiritual meaning in your love-making, your attitudes are bound to have an adverse effect on your entire marriage. They will breed resentment and a de-personalization, which will keep you apart.

ABUSE

For some—usually adolescent girls from poorer families—rape and molestation are a constant threat.

One little girl, while at home for a week, was raped every night for ten rupees a night, and she then gave the money to her mother so she could feed her little brothers.

"Did you like it?" I asked her.

"No, I didn't like it, no," she replied.

"Would you keep on doing it to get the ten rupees for your brothers?"

"Yes, I would do that," she said. "I suppose I could get used to it."

"If I gave you the ten rupees instead, to feed your brothers," I said, "would you still go to that boy?"

"No, no, no," she said, "I couldn't."

I told her it was a terrible thing the boy did to you. Anyone who comes near you again to do this, you must fight them and not allow it to happen. It was wrong, but there is nothing wrong with you. You are a very good child, and you must keep that inside your heart, no matter what happens.

There is never any scolding. They simply need to understand, because many of these children end up feeling that they are bad.

Two small girls from the school, their mother dead, were living in a little hovel somewhere in the city. We discovered that when the father went out to work he would lock them up in the hut and give the key to his neighbour to keep an eye on them. He, of course, would unlock the door and make use of them.

We sent for the father who broke down and cried. He agreed that we would keep them safe at school, and he could visit them whenever he wanted.

Whenever this kind of thing happened to the girls, I would make as little fuss as possible. The more you talk and fuss over it and say how terrible it was, the more it's driven into their minds. Make little of it, but be sure to fix it up for them so that it will never ever happen to them again. I don't encourage that age group to think and talk and be interviewed about it, because it can become a much bigger thing in their lives. I tell them it was something that happened, but now they can forget about it and let it go.

I had two sisters at school, thirteen and fourteen years old, whose father was a clerk in the local court and the mother did domestic work. A lady had come to their slum and told the mother that the girls were very pretty and that she could give them some work for one night a month for a few hundred rupees. They were taken to a place in the city where they were served nice tea with other young girls, after which they were sent home.

Then one time, an elderly gentleman took one of the girls into a bedroom and took off all her clothes. The girl gave a vivid description of the event, and I asked her how she felt.

"Very dirty," she said.

"Why do you feel dirty?" I asked her. "Surely the man who did this to you should feel dirty. What did you do with the money you got?"

"My daddy and mummy drank it," she said.

"Bring in your daddy and mummy tomorrow," I ordered.

The next day, they came in with their two girls and I wiped the floor with them. If I'd allowed my anger to really show, I'd have beaten the father up. I made the mother promise she wouldn't sell her girls any longer, and the father promised to get off the drink. I brought the girls into school as boarders.

The girls did very well until they went home for a holiday, and only one of them returned to school. Later on, the girl went home for another holiday, and she died.

Whether they killed her because she resisted them, I don't know.

There was absolutely nothing we could do.

Very often, rape also occurs in the well-off families, where extended family members are all living together. The young uncles come to them in the night, and there is nothing the girls can do because they are in the in-laws' house. The mother, an outsider, has no rights and is loath to upset anyone, so she just gives her daughter a slap and tells her not to say anything.

So, we have them primed to not tell their mummy, but when he does come to them in the night, SCREAM!

Open your mouth and scream as loud as you can, and keep screaming at the top of your voice until everyone comes running to you, and then tell them all, tell them, I was so frightened he came to me in the night, and every night he comes to me, and I get so frightened!

This kind of male behaviour flourishes in secrecy. No man like that wants to be shamed in public, so shame him, and then he'll keep away.

We do everything we can to protect our girls, and most of them learn to take care of themselves. I remember one day two Loreto girls were followed in the street by a man who kept passing remarks to them. One of the girls turned around and hit him as hard as she could across the face and told him to get away or she'd call the police.

Another Loreto girl from one of the well-off families told me that every day a man came to her and tried to talk to her. She always refused, but what really frightened her was when she came out of her house and saw him waiting for her. While she was telling me the story, she saw him standing right outside the school gates, so I rang up the police.

They arrived within ten minutes and dragged the man into school. We showed him to all the students and told them to report him to us if they ever saw the man near the school in the future.

When we got into my office, the police kicked him across the room so hard he hit the far wall. I never found out what happened after that. We never saw the man again, but he probably got a few days in jail.

INTERLUDE

THREE STUDENTS AND LOVE

A: Love is friendship. I felt it once, but it was a one-sided love because the boy only flirted with me. I loved him very much, and I still do, but he doesn't. He just passes the time with me, that's all. But I still remember him.

B: Flirting is not fun, it's selfish. Because a boy who flirts—if you fall in love with him—after a few times, he says to you, "Sorry, I was only flirting with you," and our hearts are broken. If someone comes to flirt with me or my friends, I will never really believe them or trust people in the future who really love me.

My first love broke my heart, so now I have lots of boyfriends. I'm very busy now, always busy.

C: If you fall in love, you'll know what it is. There are two kinds of feelings for love; sometimes we are very happy, but sometimes we are very sad.

But we need sadness, otherwise, without it we can't enjoy the happiness. Without happiness, we cannot tolerate sadness.

When we want something, we ask God and He will give it to us. He's like a friend to me, He always listens to me, and what I want from Him, He always gives to me. If God didn't love us, He wouldn't have created us.

SISTER CYRIL'S SAYINGS THAT THE STUDENTS REMEMBER MOST

1) Be yourself; don't do what others are doing.
2) I can teach you, but I can't put the knowledge inside your brain.
3) Don't hide your friend's faults; help her by telling her that she was wrong in what she did.
4) It doesn't matter what background you come from; the only thing that matters is what you do.
5) It is easier to wake the ones who are actually sleeping than to wake the ones who are pretending to sleep.
6) The gum-chewing girl and the cud-chewing cow are somewhat alike but different somehow; it's the look of intelligence on the cow.
7) If the door is closed, it's meant to stop the cats from coming in, not you.
8) Be honest and believe in yourself.
9) We learn from our mistakes, not by hiding them.

10) Failures pave the way to success.

11) Always do your best, and God will do the rest.

12) Do not run away when you see me; I am not a lion that'll eat you up.

13) Remember the things you've studied; don't be bothered about the parts you haven't.

14) If you've never made a mistake, you've never done anything.

15) People don't change by making resolutions; they only change when they get an insight.

16) Don't waste your time worrying about the questions you can't answer.

17) You have to go in through their door and come out through your door.

18) God is too big ever to be done.

PART VIII

Thoughts on All Kinds of Things

Happiness

Gifts and Humility

Truth and Lies

Communication

Independent Thinking

The Inside and Outside of a Person

Difficult Babies

Unsolvable Problems

HAPPINESS

When you're happy, you make other people happy.

When you're happy, you don't engage in fights or shoot your neighbour.

You only do that when you're frightened or angry.

Happiness means being fulfilled and content within yourself.

When you're young, you want to shout and sing for joy; nowadays, I do that within myself!

It is a wonderful feeling to be content. Out under trees, lovely green grass, cool air and primroses, going up through the woods, looking for fairies. When I was very tiny my father used to take me through the woods and say, "See, look, under that stone. See, look! Oh you missed him, just under that little bluebell, he's gone, see, see."

Then in our garden he would make me little seats under the bushes so I could sit and look up and see the birds, play with my dolls and my cat and dog, and watch out for the fairies.

Then riding on my Lambretta on those lovely cool winter days in Kolkata, with the breeze on my face and the clear blue sky above, I'm full of the joy of being alive and filled with gratitude towards God for such peace and good health and the opportunity to do some good to people, especially the very poor ones.

Looking back, it seems to me that happiness has been a sense of wellbeing swelling up into fantastic joy at times, but never falling below that quiet contentment of knowing that I am secure in God's hands.

Happiness also presupposes an absence of suspicion. When we are suspicious of others, we have to be constantly checking to make sure they are not cheating us. So we can never relax, we are always on edge and it is so futile, because if people want to cheat us they will find ways to do so, especially because our suspicion spoils the relationship and challenges people to do precisely what the "suspicious" expect of them.

For example, I know a school where people were left free to get on with their own work as they thought best. They were a happy staff because they were trusted and they measured up to the trust with work of a high standard. The children of the school grew up in this atmosphere of freedom and a spirit of happiness prevailed. No one counted the hours but gave freely of their time, knowing that the management would give them time if they were in need. The rules were there but as guidelines, not as chains, and it was rare that they needed to be invoked.

Then the management changed and suspicion took over. People were held strictly to timing. Lesson plans had to be handed in, although they were never looked at, just signed. Those in charge took to patrolling the school to ensure that the teachers were on their toes all the time. The fact that they had always been on their toes was not recognized by the new management, and the constant supervision sent a very strong message that they were no longer trusted, which killed their joy.

So, in less than a year, this vibrant, happy community was transformed by suspicion into a group of individuals who continued to teach, but without that inner spark which lit up their classes.

If this continues, these highly self-motivated teachers will slowly join the ranks of so many in schools all over India who require supervision to do their work, who are dependent on forces outside themselves to act and whose pupils will grow up in the same way.

Those who bring about such changes only feel secure when they are in control.

GIFTS AND HUMILITY

I've noticed when some people get up and give a talk on something, they often preface it with false humility, saying they're feeling dreadful today, or they don't know where to start, or it's all last minute and they're not really prepared.

It irritates me because it's false. I don't think they feel these things at all. They're just saying it because they don't want their audience to think they're proud.

If you're good at something, say it.

Unfortunately, I was taught early on in life, don't volunteer even if you are good. The novice mistress at the convent was looking for someone who could teach drawing, and I put my hand up and said I was good at drawing and could teach it. She looked at me as if I had committed a big social gaffe and asked if I had done drawing in school. Well, I explained, I gave it up because it clashed with my other work. So she chose someone else for the job.

It made me feel as if I was incapable and unworthy.

It took me some time to realize that people don't expect you to say you're good at something. They expect you to say, oh no, I'm not good at all, I couldn't possibly be.

It made me feel false because I knew I was good at drawing, and games, lots of things.

Why shouldn't I say I'm good at it?

I have been given my gifts in my life, and I need to use them as much as possible for others. My gifts don't function well if I use them for myself.

I think this explains this whole organization, Loreto.

The girls here are very confident. It is not an arrogance.

What's so beautiful is that you go into a class and ask who's good at drawing, and they say, Sheila's good, Mary's good, too, or I'm not good at drawing but I'm good at singing.

They know what they're good at, and they know what they're not good at. And they're not ashamed of either.

Humility is truth. The truth.

They can appreciate each other's goodness, which I think is a gift. There is no jealousy, no putting each other down.

It is very powerful.

It relates very much to your childhood and how your parents handled you and the way your teachers handled you in class.

I once had a Biology class where the teacher used to come in and ask us many questions, and when I would try to answer them, she would say, "Don't answer, you're not supposed to know the answers!" She wanted to reduce us to a state of ignorance so we could all drink in her wisdom!

That kind of thing is designed to flatten out young children for the rest of their lives.

You get a gift of sweets from someone. What do you do? You can put it in a nicely wrapped box and say I don't have any sweets, or you can go around and offer them to everyone.

I believe our gifts are given to us to use for others and not to hide.

TRUTH AND LIES

There was a girl from the Netherlands who stayed in one of our guest rooms on the top floor of the school. She left her purse and passport on her bed and locked her door. When she returned, she found they had been taken, but the door was still locked.

I sent for all the children, explained what had happened and told them if any of them had any suspicions to come and see me. By the evening, two of them came and told me when they had been studying outside the toilets, one of the girls had gone in and stayed a very long time. When she eventually came out, she went straight to the statue of Our Lady in the corridor, then disappeared downstairs.

When we looked behind the statue, we found the purse and passport, but I wanted to discover how the student had done it. I told a tall, thin girl, Podho, to go through the ventilator shaft in the toilet to see if it was possible to get into the rooms. It was.

I called the other girl to my office and asked her what she had done with the stolen things. She denied everything and cried. I told her that we knew all about it and to tell me the truth. It took a long time, but she finally confessed.

What did I do?

I hugged her, a big hug, and told her I was very proud of her for telling the truth. She was a child, I knew, who had stolen things for many, many years, but I think the idea that she could get a hug and be forgiven helped her a lot.

I recently found out that she married into a good Catholic family and has a beautiful daughter.

Even when we are young children, we know right from wrong, truth from lies. It's programmed into us by our parents and the environment we grow up in.

I also knew right from wrong in my childhood, but I went through a whole period in my noviceship where I unfortunately learnt to tell lies.

I remember the nuns asking me what my principal fault was—I was barely seventeen, and I hadn't got a clue—and I told them I was very quick, so I could be very impatient with people, and that I forgot things easily.

I have a photographic memory, but I forget simple things like giving out messages. So after that, I was given any sort of job that involved remembering what I was supposed to be doing, and I would find myself forgetting it, and I would quickly cover up my tracks by lying so I wouldn't get caught.

My noviceship was not so very holy.

I soon realized how stupid all of that was, so I stopped it completely, but it gave me an insight into children who are frightened and tell lies because they're afraid.

For me, it wasn't so much being afraid as not wanting to get caught, and it linked in strongly with me being a Number 3 (those who crave success) on the Enneagram.

At Loreto, there was a time when things went missing from the teachers' lockers: biscuits, snacks, money. One evening, we discovered one of our girls, who had just arrived straight from the street, helping herself to someone's locker, and later found all kinds of things she'd accumulated in her locker. Many of the young children off the street did this when they first arrived at Loreto, and the only basic rule they had to learn was: respect other people's property.

At one point, it was happening so much that I decreed that all the lockers in school be left open to place everybody on an honest plane.

If you're raiding someone's locker, someone else might be raiding yours! If everyone agreed to be honest, I told them, then everything would be fine. Not long after, all the littlest junior students—all around table height and below—arrived one morning in the courtyard with lipstick smeared all over their faces, all caught there and then having raided the big girls' lockers!

The rule was always if anybody stole anything, nobody went home from that class until it was found. Most of the time things were returned.

Whatever you take in life, you return.

But what about the lies that people tell almost without thinking... Lies before an election, promises when some politician is making a speech and tells everyone that he intends to set up some free scheme for feeding the poor. Does he really have the intention and then forgets, or is he really sincere and then later cannot deliver for reasons outside his control? Or is he just plain lying?

If you look at truth and lies among bureaucrats, the first thing you notice is that they are not all at it—only some of them are corrupt—and most of the time at a level where the salary is poor, which encourages people to make a little on the side.

But if you look at the top politicians, that's a very different crowd.

Most of them in Parliament have assets of more than 50 crore (7 million GBP), and many of them have acquired their assets through politics—there's no other way they could have done it. And when you think of the sheer poverty that surrounds them! Of course, as long as they pay their taxes, they can't be caught. It's mind-boggling. The country could have lovely roads and lots of good employment if the money was used well.

The Chief Minister of Uttar Pradesh in the early 2000s had statues of herself built all over Lucknow, and in every one of them she's holding her little handbag. She came into power in Uttar Pradesh just after I left there, so we were never there at the same time, but over the years, I've returned over and over and seen for myself these obscene structures. I think she's tried to make her city resemble the President's Palace in Delhi—huge blocks of stone everywhere.

The large square in Lucknow, the Maidan, was originally a space even bigger than the one we have in Kolkata, but she filled it up with roads, ceremonial arches, and stone blocks of herself holding that handbag. Right across from the Maidan are the poor living in the most dreadful hovels you can imagine. No electricity, nothing. But at night, she had the park and her statues lit up, so bright it looked like daylight.

To my knowledge, she never built one single thing for the poor while in power. Ah, to have wasted such an opportunity as that! But unfortunately, nobody was allowed close enough to her to ask her any difficult questions, to face her with the truth. She had surrounded herself with sycophants, and there was no one to challenge her.

I sometimes ask myself, if I had been in Lucknow while she was there, what would I have done?

I think I would have found a way to sit down with her and have a long talk...

COMMUNICATION

For me, communication comes on many different levels. If I'm communicating with God, nothing is held back because he sees me from the inside. But if I meet someone on the stairs who I don't know, we smile at each other and say something, but I'm not revealing myself at all, just being nice. In between those extremes are all your different levels where you decide how much you want to communicate to others about yourself.

At Loreto, I always meet the teachers every morning and tell them everything that is happening in the school, keeping all the lines open so whatever is done is transparent, so people can understand not just what you're doing but why.

If I see a child crying in the playground, I'll call her over and ask her what happened, why she's upset. And ultimately, we'll probably sit down and talk it through. Maybe she's crying because her mother is very sick, or someone died in her family, so my communication would be putting my arms around her, holding her, praying for her within myself.

It would depend on the circumstances, but I firmly believe being able to talk to and explain things to people is very important.

The other aspect of communication is listening and keeping yourself available. When we don't listen, we cut off communication, and because of our body language, the way we're looking at them, our facial expressions, a single word can block things. If they've had a bad experience, they often don't feel like communicating with us at all, so all of this becomes very important.

One thing we should remember, though, is that we often jump to conclusions and judge people too quickly. When we meet someone for the first time, it's very possible that they just happen to be having a bad day and are angry, but from then on we always think of them as bad-tempered.

We should give people enough time to grow. We should allow them the freedom to be different.

INDEPENDENT THINKING

My zoological background has stood me in good stead over the years. It has enabled me to teach, but it's more than that, because when you write a doctorate and do your thesis, you learn how to think and organize material, how to select what should go in and what shouldn't, and how to write it. My thesis was on reproductive thyroid endocrinology in the Indian house gecko. A thesis has to say something, it needs an argument within it and it needs to prove that this is the way things happen.

It's very important that children learn to think independently for themselves, not simply to believe in superstitions or statements that are made, but to be able to find the proof about what's been said. Otherwise you believe, but nothing else.

It's true that we believe a lot of stuff simply on faith, but there are many things we believe in that are, strictly speaking, not true.

You read a newspaper. Do you believe everything it says? You read a second paper and it says the opposite. We do sessions with our Class 9 and 10 students, where we give them five or six different newspapers and get them to compare the same article in each paper, and they learn very quickly how different versions of the same story can come about. In the next lesson, I do an exercise where I describe a riot taking place in a school because nobody was allowed out in time for lunch. I give the students different roles: a student, a father, an outsider, a reporter in the street, a parent not involved in the action. I tell them that each group is going to report from their own point of view on the riot.

The students soon perceive how different their descriptions were of what was going on and how different was the sense of injustice about the events. This enables young people to recognize how one's perception colours what one writes. This gets the students thinking and helps them to be able to recognize manipulative writing.

There was a famous writer from Bangladesh who was given refuge here in Kolkata, and certain people in the Muslim community orchestrated a riot because the West Bengal Government said they would allow her to settle here permanently, and these people didn't want that. So they fed the story to the media that she had blasphemed against the Koran. Many adolescent boys came out in angry crowds to shout slogans against her, yet on being questioned, they admitted that they had never read anything written by her. She had never blasphemed, but people believed it and acted on it.

We must teach our children to think for themselves and not just act blindly, follow someone's orders.

A Class 10 girl told me her friends were studying at a government computer college and she needed 500 rupees (5 GBP) as a deposit. At the end of the course, if you've been present for every class and you pass all the exams, you got the money back. I gave her the money, and six months later, she came back with a large computer book and gave me back the 500 rupees.

I have many similar stories, which convinced me that when children reach a certain level in their development, usually at around fifteen to seventeen years of age, they want to take control of their own lives, and they don't need someone else hanging around telling them what to do. Let them get on and find themselves.

Next to the school was an apartment where the older students would stay and live. One time, I felt it necessary to bring back some of the younger students to school because they weren't ready, accountable or responsible enough to live there, which they didn't like at all and complained about.

One of them, though, told me she had found another apartment near the Red Light district, and she needed a letter from me to allow her a place in the hostel. I found it was run by a lady who catered to girls who wished to leave prostitution and instead go to college. I wrote the letter, and since then, many of my students have stayed at that hostel and received all kinds of college training, and it has shown me how many of them can take control of their lives without my help.

There is confidence within them that they are free, that even if they make a mistake, they are not going to be condemned by us.

I say, make your mistakes, and I'll accept them.

Don't depend on me.

THE INSIDE AND OUTSIDE OF A PERSON

We clothe the outside of ourselves with so many things, we make an impression on people, but it doesn't mean we're the same person inside at all.

When we meet a person, we don't really know them, because people meet each other from behind a mask and have to make sure the other person likes us and is ready to accept us, have that person believe in us. And only when we get really close do we feel secure that we are accepted, and only then do we really reveal ourselves. Otherwise we always keep something back.

Of course, the other person is doing the same. It's a bit of a game.

When I see kids going off to America and returning with an American accent, "Where did you get that accent?" I ask. "Because I know you grew up here in Kolkata." I know some of them put it on because they want people to know where they've been.

It takes time to get to the inside, but I think it's the most important place. The inside is the real you, the outside is the veneer you put on to make you acceptable to others.

As for myself, I've never much thought about the outside as long as my inside was alright, with regards to being neat and tidy.

One day, I was out with the children on a retreat and sent them out to find a symbol of nature which would tell them what God thought of them. I went out to check on them and came across a beautiful palm tree, tall and slim, and I thought, this is my symbol.

And then I realized, in truth, it was not.

So I went a little further on and found a banana tree. Now, if you look at a banana tree, its leaves hang out in all directions, a bit shredded and squalid-looking, so I said to myself, "Ah, this is my symbol, I'm like the banana tree!"

No one is really bad. There's always something good inside. Last year, I was in Canada, and every night I had dinner with a group of men who were out on parole living in a special house run by a Jesuit, and each of them took turns cooking for all of us. They had been felons of all different kinds—a couple of them were murderers!—but I found them the most loving people I'd met for a long time, and I felt completely at home with them.

I made friends with them, and I think one of the things about that group of men was that their insides were all on the outside, they put on no airs and graces to influence or impress me. They were just themselves.

DIFFICULT BABIES

Good news doesn't make money. People don't read the newspapers in order to read the good news; they read them for the sensational stuff. People do bad things, but you ask yourself, what made them like that? Where do they come from? What kind of background do they have? When I probed the backgrounds of the parolees I had dinner with, I discovered all of them had dysfunctional families.

The only thing we are born with is our temperament.

There are easy babies, and there are difficult babies. If you are born with an easy disposition, every time someone picks you up you gurgle, and so people respond to you. People's responses to you are a mirror image of what you are presenting to them. The easy babies grow up with adults who like them, there is a realization that they're liked, and so the world is a positive place.

Difficult babies cry and wince when they're picked up, so what they get from adults is a corresponding reaction, and they won't seem very loving at all towards the child. So these children grow up feeling the world is against them, and every time they meet someone, they look at them with suspicion rather than openness.

At the refuge in Canada, there were two Indians from a refugee camp for victims of war. When they were nine and twelve years old respectively, they had become separated from their mother and taken to a Mennonite organization in Canada where they were adopted. They spoke no English, couldn't communicate at all, and by the time they were fifteen years old, they were on the street selling drugs when they were picked up and put in jail.

Since those days, one of them has become a Christian—his father had been a priest in Indonesia—and is about to go to university. A lot can depend on the opportunity we give children when they are young, and it's one of the reasons I work with street kids.

I've seen my kids in Kolkata blossom from mice to well-educated young women, so, no, I don't believe the world is all bad.

Some of the very worst are at the top. When I think of the American government wanting to rain down fire on Syria because they used chemical weapons! The Americans themselves have used chemical weapons on half a dozen separate occasions, but that is quietly forgotten. It's those people I would want to tackle if I had anything to do with it, which I don't! But, I do pray for them, and I hope that God will touch their souls with some grace and make them more human.

The world is what we make of it, but I do think there must have been a lot of difficult babies born, yes...

UNSOLVABLE PROBLEMS

One problem I come across quite frequently is when the father and mother get divorced. The father has gone off with another woman or the wife has gone off with another man, and they've both remarried and had children of their own, and the children who are left behind from the broken marriage are asking, please God, bring mummy and daddy back together again, make my family whole again.

Can God do it?

No. Because if He does, He'll have two more families asking the same thing.

Unsolvable problem?

So, how do we handle that kind of problem with the children here?

I simply say to them, listen, God is not there to solve all your problems, but He'll give you the strength to cope with them. So sit down, cry your eyes out to Him about your mummy and daddy, and slowly, slowly, slowly, after some time, you'll feel strength coming into you, and you'll feel ready and able to cope without your mummy and daddy.

That's what God can do for you. That's how He solves problems.

Everything is in God's hands! Everything, but we have to take action.

I know a teacher who used to have this extremely bad situation in her house, whereby the landlord wanted to throw them all out onto the street. This had been going on for a long, long time. At the last minute, she came to me for help, and we went down to her house late one night, and I asked her why had she not told me about the problem earlier when I could have taken some real action for her. Well, she said, I was sure God would solve the problem.

I stamped all over the place and felt like strangling her there and then on the pavement—it was God's mercy I didn't do it. Can you imagine anything as silly as that?! She had sat there for three months letting people walk all over her, when she could have taken proper legal action.

If you want His help, take His strength with you, and solve your own problems.

INTERLUDE

A PRISON JOKE...

This fellow went to prison, and the first night there, he was sitting at the dinner table, when all of a sudden one prisoner got up, shouted out: "125!" And everyone laughed. Then another got up, shouted out: "247!" And again, everyone laughed.

So, the new fellow quietly asked his neighbour what was going on, and he said, "Well, we've all been here so long and we know everyone so well that we've numbered all the jokes to save ourselves the trouble of having to tell them."

"Great," the new one said. "Can I try?"

So he boldly got up, shouted out "783!!!" And no one laughed.

Embarrassed, he turned to his neighbour and asked, "What's wrong? Is there no joke with that number?"

His neighbour replied, "There's a joke all right, but you told it all wrong."

FREEDOM

Freedom is the ability to regulate oneself

Freedom does not require supervision

Freedom is doing one's duty, even when no one is looking

Freedom is not being afraid to speak

Freedom is being able to be oneself—on the outside as the inside

Freedom is being left free to do a job your own way

Freedom always presupposes responsibility

Freedom removes tension and enables a person to give her best

Freedom has to set it own limits—our conscience tells us what they are

Freedom is not to be taken advantage of

Freedom allows us to learn from our mistakes, not hide them

Freedom is doing what one has to do, because one believes in it

THREE STUDENTS TALK ABOUT THEIR LIVES

A: I'm twelve years old. Loreto Sealdah is a very good school; we learn how to share with people, how to behave with everyone. Our teachers help the poor a lot, and we help them to help the poor. I can't think of anything that is difficult about our school. If you're learning then nothing is difficult. We try, so nothing else is really important for us. We love coming here and being with our friends and learning all kinds of new activities.

It takes me one and a half hours to come here by bus, three hours every day.

B: I'm eleven years old. I live in a small house with my sister and mother and father. She's also in this school. My father and mother help me a lot with my studies. My mother is my best friend, and I share everything with her. If I have any problems, even serious ones, I go ahead and tell her. I feel comfortable with her. We enjoy each other a lot. If it's a serious problem, she'll give me the solution to it.

My favourite word is sharing—friendship.

Friendships are important because friends can support us in any given situation and help in us in every way. We should try and share even if they're not friends.

We have a huge population, but compared to that, the food we produce is very low, so we need to increase the quantity and quality to help people more. If the prices go up, poor people cannot eat.

C: I'm eight. I want to become a doctor, a child specialist. Children are very sweet, and my doctor talks to me very sweetly. He is very kind. I saw him last year because I had a cough and a cold. I'm okay now.

I have one cousin, a brother and a sister, and they all live in Kolkata. I live about a half hour from here. I come here sometimes by bus, sometimes by bicycle, sometimes by taxi.

I like pink; I have a pink dress which I bought. It's beautiful.

I have a small, soft dolphin toy at home in my bedroom. It's quite big. That's my favourite.

PART IX

Thoughts on Myself

WHAT DID I IMAGINE ALL THOSE YEARS AGO?

People keep asking me what plans I've got for the future. What am I going to do next?

I don't know what I'm going to do next. I do what God provides for me. I seize the opportunities He puts before me.

Did I imagine any of this when I was a small girl? No, never. I just lived my life, played games, did lessons like other children, had my dog and my cat, did a lot of swimming, played tennis in the summers, went fishing, went for long, long bike rides with my friends.

It wasn't always easy, we weren't rich, it was the Second World War, but unlike every other child in our town who lived on that awful black bread, my father had contacts out in the country, and he would go out and get an unauthorized sack of wheat, grind it up in a little coffee grinder, and my mother would make this beautiful brown soda bread.

We kept a lovely jersey cow called Dolly out on the edge of town. Unfortunately, when she was in calf, she got milk fever, we couldn't get the milk out of her fast enough because she was producing so much of it, and she died. This happened when I was nine. On my way home from school someone ran up to me and shouted, "Dolly's dead, Dolly's dead!" I came home in floods of tears. My brother took me to the cowshed where she was lying and with some scissors he cut off all the lovely little curls around her face, put them inside an envelope with Dolly's name on it and the date, then gave it to me to keep always. I was consoled.

I think my brother was a wonderful psychologist.

I got my strength from Dolly's milk, which is why I've got good, strong bones.

I love Ireland, I'll never give it up, but I love India, too. It's become a part of me and my life. I love going back to Ireland, I still have lots of friends there, but I wouldn't want to live there for good. Not anymore. It's lovely to go back for a holiday because you're a bit of a celebrity there, but if you live there for good you become a bit of a nuisance.

The wood of Kilruddery was the place I used to see the fairies. It was one of those big estates taken by the British by driving the poor Irish off their land. It was just up the road from us, and we had a free run of the land. The owners never disturbed us. It had a big wall all around, and we crossed two fields at the back of our house, climbed the wall and were into the woods and the magic. There was a main gate, too, but it was more magical to get into the woods the other way.

One of the places had a lovely walk up through the woods, with ornamental gardens and all that stuff, and on Sunday mornings my father used to carry me on his shoulders while I held on to his head. We went up, up, up, and climbed right up to the top of Brayhead and looked straight out across the Irish Sea to Wales.

I've been back to that same spot many times. It's still unchanged, although all around it has been built up. The home I grew up in was passed on to someone else by my father, who passed away long ago, but every time I go by there, I remember it all even though it was over sixty years ago.

In those days, we could go for lovely walks, and you'd never find anything destroyed. A lot of those areas have now been closed off because of the vandalism by young people. Nowadays, kids seem to destroy things just for the satisfaction of destroying them. They even set fire to places just for the fun of seeing them burn.

How much parental training goes into bringing children up?

In most families both parents work and have little time to talk to and influence children. So they spend a lot of time in front of the television—it substitutes for other activities in their free time—from which they often imbibe very dubious values, which express themselves in destructive behaviour when they are left on their own.

Children are not being reared to entertain themselves creatively.

MY FIRST JOURNEY TO INDIA

Starting out at DunLaoire in Ireland, then by ferry across the Irish Sea to Hollyhead, and a train to London—my first time out of Ireland, at age seventeen! I still remember the Sisters who were taking us. They had left Ireland in the early 1930s, and this was their first visit back after more than twenty years. What courage! What commitment!

I can still feel the train wheels going clickity-click on the tracks all the way down to London, where we arrived in the early morning. My only memory of the city is Marks and Spencer, where my companion and I spent our time riding up and down on the escalators (the first we had ever seen in our lives), while the older Sisters window-shopped to their hearts' content. (They had no money!)

We sailed from Southampton on the tide at midnight by which time we were tucked into our berths and fast asleep, so when we came up on deck in the morning we were well out to sea. Our time on board was spent reading, talking, walking, praying, and watching the people around us. Then one evening, it got dark so suddenly, I shouted out loud, to the great amusement of my companions, who informed me that we had just crossed into the tropics. Apart from watching the flying fish and seeing the occasional whale, the only other excitement was when we reached Cape Town.

We were already in port when we came up on deck to see Table Mountain with its tablecloth of mist. Drawn up on the quay were two buses for those who wished to go sightseeing, one marked "Whites" and one "Non-whites".

My first exposure to apartheid.

We had been all mixed together on the boat, Europeans, Africans, Indians, no one conscious of colour, enjoying ourselves. Thank God, our Loreto Sisters from Strand came to take us to spend the day with them, but it was difficult to forget apartheid. Going back in the '90s almost forty years later, after the first free elections, I was struck to see a white co-pilot holding the door for his black pilot to pass through first!

Two events from that first visit stand out in my memory: the time I fell into the Indian Ocean trying to take a photograph, and the time I caused great amusement by announcing excitedly that I had seen giraffes and zebras grazing in a field!

It took us three days to sail around the Cape and into Durban. Here we met an Irish widow and her daughter who drove us 70 miles to the Valley of a Thousand Hills. The hills were really vertical folds all around what looked like an extinct volcano, and the people lived in little huts tucked into the folds. The children came up to school on the edge of the crater, and I saw boys playing football in their bare feet for the first time. On our way back we stopped at a huge monastery, which had a very well-equipped vocational training workshop to educate the African boys from the nearby farms, so as to improve their methods of farming, even though the monks had been ordered by the Government not to educate the Zulu boys. Again, when I went back forty years later, the whole place was a hive of activity.

The biggest miracle, of course, was the peacefulness.

While I was there on my second visit, I talked to the cook who looked after us in our hostel. She had deep furrows down her arms and legs, and when I asked, she explained that when she was a child and Nelson Mandela was put in jail, all the children came out on the streets to protest. The police had put out huge rolls of barbed wire, and they would shoot over the heads of the children, who would then run in fear through the barbed wire and get cut all over. In the evening the police would come and take all the children who were cut, put them in jail, and beat the boys the whole night long.

The girls were locked up and had to listen to the boys screaming.

I said to her, "How can you stand here and talk so peacefully to me when white people have done this to you?"

Her answer: "Mandela taught us to forgive. If we do not forgive, we will destroy ourselves..."

BEING THE BOSS

I have to make lots of decisions that are difficult to make, and there are many people who want lots of different things from me, and no one is willing to wait. I don't know if I get tired or not, but I have been blessed with energy and I can still go on and enjoy it all.

Anyone who has read books on management will know that there are many ways of being the boss, but if you examine them carefully, you will find that they can all be included under bosses who like being the boss and those who do not. In other words, those who control and those who guide.

Being the boss at Loreto Sealdah is like jumping into a pond with the water closing over your head as you go in every morning: "Excuse me, Sister, I've come to enquire..." "Please Sister, may I have some glue?" "Sister, Sister, someone fell off the roof!" "Sister, come quickly, there's a fight at the gate!" And then it's time for Assembly and the merciful quiet of the morning prayer.

But, if I was a boss of the controlling type, like the Sergeant teaching his new recruits military discipline ("When I tell you to jump, you will jump, and you'll stay up in the air until I tell you to come down again!"), I would not have so many people bothering me, as they would all be kept in control by the rules and regulations.

Basically, it all boils down to what St Paul has to say: "For those who love, the law is not necessary." We need rules for those who live by the law, as they do not understand the freedom of love. So in this context, what does being the boss mean? It means that as the boss we have two choices. We can choose the path of control, where we run our organization like a machine, where rules are kept regardless of human error or need, where everything is done by the book, no room for creativity or fun, the motivation is fear, and without supervision nothing happens. In other words, people function for reasons outside themselves.

Or we can choose the path of freedom, working together for an end everyone believes in, so there's no need for control as everyone is busy doing the work because they want to, not because they are forced.

I prefer to be a boss who makes people feel secure, who trust me totally, and vice versa. Everything we do is discussed, and even when decisions are changed, we trust each other to the extent of not doing it arbitrarily but out of necessity. We don't need endless consultations.

Trust.

And that is the difference between being the boss with the security of being in tight control, or being the boss and running the risk of leaving people free—the way God does.

ICONS

If you put someone up on a pedestal, if you make an icon out of them, then you relieve yourself from all responsibility of doing something similar to what they're doing.

Not that I would expect anyone to imitate me, but I would hope that something of what is happening here at Loreto would get across to people, in the sense that they would look out beyond themselves and see the agony of these street children, and open up their schools to welcome them and make them feel at home.

For me, it has always been simple: How can I run a lovely school with lots of nicely dressed children coming in from good homes, well fed by their parents, well looked after by the school, lots of money coming in to pay the fees, if I leave all those other little creatures out in the gutter, and forget about them? How can I live my life? How can I? How can anybody?

I do not consider myself worthy at all of all the attention I've received, because I find most of the work I get credit for was down to my staff. By myself, I can't even find a photograph of myself.

I think people see all the work that has been done, they see the results of it, the effect I seem to have on people, and I suppose they consider me worthy.

Why does anybody want to give awards to anybody? Awards can be for various reasons: to encourage people to do something, or to draw attention to the people who are giving the award so maybe they will get something out of it.

I don't know, but I find, most of the time, it's to encourage people and to recognize something good that's been done.

There are many organizations looking around for people to give awards to. If people go on Wikipedia, I suppose they'll see lots of things about me, but I don't actually know Wikipedia. People write to me all the time offering to make donations, and I tell them to send it all to Loreto Sealdah.

I can't say I don't enjoy being a celebrity, in the sense that people meet me and say hello. I don't get disturbed by it like Princess Diana did. If it happens, it happens, if it doesn't, it doesn't.

I get these awards, but I don't know what to do with them. I have one whole trunk full of them at home, and I'm not sure what to do. The Governor of West Bengal told me he's been getting all kinds of gifts for years, and he's decided to put them all into two big boxes and send them over to the school so our children can play with them...

GETTING THINGS DONE

My Golden Rules for Getting Things Done are as follows:

Always be clear about what you want done.

Talk about it beforehand so people become familiar with your ideas.

Meet individuals, then meet the whole group.

Be good at selling your own ideas to people.

Remember: getting things done means wanting to change something.

But that being said, I don't think I've really done that much. I've always had other people to do it, otherwise I couldn't possibly have done it all.

I see all challenges as positives. I like challenges, but often I'm faced with situations that can be very slow, because everyone is multi-tasking, so stuff is constantly put on hold.

Let me give an example: I go to meet the Chairman of such-and-such company because I need him to sign a cheque to get a school started. (The chairpersons are the best ones to go to—provided I can get to them, they are always in meetings—because they make the final decisions.) I've written him a letter, and when I see him in a few days, I'll sit in front of him and tell him this has to be done; can you do it? But I'll do it with grace, respect and patience, because he may not be able to do it immediately. I already know he has the money, because I've already checked up on him behind his back, but I need to get him to write it out formally so I can receive the money. I need to be sensitive to his position, because he is the chairman with lots of rupees at his fingertips, so I take care how I handle him.

I overcome with patience.

I know it will happen. It happens because I'm convinced God is with me throughout all of this, and He will eventually make it all happen. In the meantime, I do my best, pull as many strings as I can, remain sensitive to people's sensitivities, and contact as many people as I can to see who can do it best. But beneath it all, if God wants it to happen, it'll happen.

Over the years through working like this, it's happened over and over. I take no credit for being a mover and a shaker and getting people to do things.

But I do my homework. I like to be prepared, to have my reasons, and make them understandable for everyone. It's all about quiet persuasion.

Whenever I was trying to get anything done in a school—for instance, with parents—I would always have a meeting with them first, and I would talk a lot about what I wanted to do, about the possible formats, then when I felt I'd talked enough, and people had got the idea, I'd ask them if they were willing to do it, and people would hopefully begin to see the sense in my words.

When I'm trying to change things, to get something done, I never directly confront.

If you come in as a big heavyweight and say "Do it," you'll get resistance. The more powerful you are, the less overt the resistance will be, but it will be there nonetheless, underneath. You can force people to do what you want, and it will still get done, but then you never know how long it might last because there is no real contribution from the people being forced to do it. They're only doing it because they've been told to.

If you really want to affect lasting change, you need to persuade people that the particular change is for the good—for their own good or for someone else's—and only when that change takes place inside of them can it be truly lasting and sustainable.

Some people get things done for the good of others, for the good of the community, for the good of the nation, and that's great. I admire them, they're not heroes, but they're very good people.

But they have to be totally convinced about what they want to change. If they don't believe in it, no one else will.

Even then, there can be a lot of resistance. If so, I let go of the idea for the time being and just tell everyone we'll come back to it sometime in the future, and I'll make sure the next time my points are more developed, stronger, much more in my favour.

I rarely give up. If I'm convinced enough that my idea is a good one, but it's being continually rejected, I adapt it, and return the next year, then the next year, and the year after that, until people finally give in, and everyone is able to agree.

I just have to realize and accept that my original idea might have been proposed at the wrong time, or at the wrong place, or to the wrong set of people. So it's me who needs to adapt.

YOUR BEST IS ENOUGH!

Internally, I've become much calmer. I can stand back now, let things happen, and accept that not everybody has my vision. I don't need to push it on everybody I meet. If people want to take it, it's there. I can feel serene about it.

If people want to come and listen to me then this is what they'll get, and if they don't listen, whose loss is it? The children's, who they'll never get to work with. That does bother me, but I can't do much about that.

My faith has grown deeper over the years, and the fact is that all this is His work, not mine. If it goes well, He gets the credit, and if it goes badly—as long as it really isn't my fault—then it's His fault. I'm not passing on any responsibility here, I'm just doing my best, and if things don't work out, I don't have to go and commit suicide, do I? If something is so important for someone it makes them want to throw themselves under a train, well, I don't work like that, no.

The scribes in the Scriptures were fighting about whether or not Christianity would live or die, and one man stood up and said, "If this is truly from God it will survive, if not, it will die."

It survived.

Let me put it another way.

If I'm transferred tomorrow from Loreto or I drop down dead, and someone else comes in and takes charge of all this, and reduces thirty years of work to a mess, I'd think, whatever good I have succeeded in doing still exists, and can't be undone.

You do your best, to your limit, and that's enough! What more can you do? Except get stomach ulcers worrying about everything, which is why this place is relaxed.

I only give ulcers to other people when I shout because I can't get what I need done!

In the course of my time here, hopefully, I have done some good to somebody. Hopefully.

Someone else will come along after me and try and do their good. It'll be a different good to my good, but I feel whatever I can do by way of goodness I'll do, and I don't have to worry that I couldn't do all the good I wanted to or should have done.

RESCUING A CHILD: CHANDA'S STORY

Chanda. Her telephone number is in my pocket right now because I'm supposed to call her. She's grown up now, and has her own baby. She originally came from a dreadful slum at the back of Loreto Bowbazar, a place built on a garbage dump, where the huts are all built from bits and pieces of cardboard, rexine, tarpaulin, and old bricks they find in the garbage.

In all the slums of Kolkata, a cardboard box—such as you would bring your groceries home in—spread out flat on the ground makes a good bed, because it keeps the damp out. This is the level Chanda came from.

At some point, she was picked up by a German lady and put into Loreto Bowbazar as a regular student in kindergarten. The lady paid for her school fees, then put her into a boarding school until she was about ten years old. At this point, Chanda became very, very bold, so bold that the nuns wouldn't keep her. She was sent home, but Chanda's mother wouldn't take her back.

So she was brought over to me at Loreto Sealdah, and after a very short time we discovered she was an extremely good thief. During assembly, some money had been stolen from the teacher's bag while she had been looking after a line of children. The bag had been right next to her, yet the money had disappeared. We left no stone unturned to find the culprit, and then one of the other children told us he remembered Chanda sitting down beside the bag to change her shoes. And sure enough, we found out Chanda had taken the money.

Another time, she stole money, then stole my diary off my desk and hid the money inside the diary, which she then hid in my cupboard because she knew I never locked it. (I'm of the opinion if you don't lock things up, they're not worth stealing.) I had to talk to her to get it out of her and find out where the money was and also for her to admit to everything.

Anyway, she grew up, had various problems, wasn't too bad at her lessons, and when she got to Class 8, at about fourteen years of age, she fell in love with a young boy, a carpenter's son. They ran off and got married in a registry office.

Of course she wasn't of age, but ages can always be fudged!

Afterwards, she went to live with his family, where she drove them all mad by making all kinds of demands on them—she really was very bold—until finally the father came crying to me, and I told him the only thing to do was to give her a good scolding and she might be all right, which is what happened, and she settled down fine.

Later, she came back to me with her two-year-old baby, very well looked after, neat and clean and tidy, and she told me she'd already got a job but she wanted to finish her open school.

I remember when she first came to me, and then I think of her now. She's become a responsible adult with a small child, a working husband, everything is organized within a settled family. She is no longer on the street, no longer in a slum.

And I think to myself, our intervention made a difference to that child.

A SHORT TOUR OF KOLKATA WITH SISTER DRIVING

This interview was conducted in the school minivan, while driving around the insane streets of Kolkata.

Sister Cyril: We have to be going now. I'll go anywhere in the world that you want me to take you. (She revs up the engine and adjusts her starched, white habit.) Shall we drive aimlessly around, from place to place or what? (The school gates open to a cacophony of noisy street traffic.)

Neil Farrelly: Is there any point putting on a seat belt?

SC: (Signalling right) We have to wait for this traffic. (Shouting across to the gatemen) Hey! Stop the traffic for me! (Her car passes through the gates onto Netaji Subhash Chandra Bose Road: screeching brakes, squealing tyres, continuous honking horns.) So, ask me some questions.

NF: What do you want your epitaph to be?

SC: Something like the founder of our congregation, "To live with the poor, to die with the poor, and to rise with the poor was ever the aim of Mary Ward." So, I think: "As long as you did it to one of the least of my brothers, you did it to me." That's what I'd say. I live by that.

(11:04 am, stuck in traffic, hundreds of yellow taxis, motorbikes, and blue and yellow buses stretching down the street).

NF: What do you think is the biggest obstacle in life for the rich?

SC: Money and possessions. Easier for a camel to pass through the eye of a needle than for a rich man to get into heaven, Jesus said. It's difficult when you're used to good things and comfort and enjoyment to give them all up.

There's a group of Christians—I won't mention names—who don't try to make converts out of the Hindus, but what they do is when they find a destitute Catholic family, they befriend them, get their kids into good schools, organize scholarships for them, get the mother and father jobs, and when they're all settled, they say, if you want to continue like this, you need to become a part of us.

If you're destitute, it's easier to say no, but if your children are in good schools, it's much harder to do so.

Look, there's the Catholic graveyard over there on the left, and I forgot to show you Mother Teresa's place back there, and here's another building going up—I don't know if they have planning permission for that or not.

NF: Ready for another question?

SC: Have I answered the last one?

NF: I think so. Do you want to say anything else?

SC: No, but there are two things about money. One of them is status, your standing in society, and the fact that people respect you if you have money, that has a big part to play. The other is that you have all the comforts in life. And power.

NF: Who do you think is doing good in the world today?

SC: Everyone is doing some form of "good," unless they're doing bad. There's nothing neutral about this. Many people are just living their life, keeping well, keeping to the rules and laws, not hurting their neighbours, but for me, in our current situation, it's not enough.

They're the silent majority, and they allow bad to be done by their inertia. They don't take action, and they should take action.

There are a lot of bullies out there that should not be allowed to bully! They can't bully so much in Kolkata—there's a strong community spirit here—because the local population would tear them to pieces, but they target individual groups.

Look, the Archbishop's house is over there, and another church, and another, and St Xavier's College.

(Quite suddenly, we're moving down a tree-lined avenue with cleaner air.)

NF: Quite posh here, isn't it?

SC: Oh yes, all these schools are posh here, even our school is posh without the children.

NF: What do you mean?

SC: With the children, it's dirty because they drop litter and do all the things children normally do.

NF: But compared to the rest of India, your school's clean.

SC: Yes, it's okay, and anyway, cleanliness is relative.

Now, that road down there goes to Loreto House, but we're not going down there. This is the top end of Park Street, it's one way.

NF: Is it true that at a certain time of day in Kolkata, the whole road system changes direction?

SC: Yes. At 2:00 pm. Up until then, all the traffic flows east to west, but by 2:00 o'clock—or it could be 1:00 o'clock, I'm not sure—the traffic changes and it all flows from west to east, and the result is that you need to know how to get around in the afternoon.

NF: Tricky.

SC: I'm not kidding, you need to know your roads...

Look, there's the beautiful St Paul's Cathedral. A lot of what you see around here was built by the British.

(Stopped again in solid traffic, light-headed from the carbon monoxide; a man is walking down the middle of the road selling towels.) Here, look, I don't like these big, fat local buses on the road climbing all over you. They're dangerous, but I have to say when I put my hand up for them to stop, they do stop.

NF: More questions?

SC: Yes, yes, of course.

NF: What's the best sandwich combination?

SC: Tomatoes and onions, a little cheese, and to be really deluxe, add some salmon and a few other things that you can't ever get here. (Doing a U-turn) We're going left; I'm going to take you another way under the big roadway.

NF: What kind of cheese?

SC: In India, there is only one cheese, Amul cheese. I like all cheddar cheeses, but I don't like the smelly French cheeses. They're a little bit off, you know.

On the right of us here is a big film complex. Oh no, I'm in the wrong lane again, I need to turn around. Let's wait for the light to change. (Next to our car, a chai wallah is serving tea to two customers.)

NF: What do you say to people who believe nothing changes, and there is no point in doing anything?

SC: If you say there is no point, then nothing will change and your prophesy will come absolutely true. But if you say yes, then something always changes, always, always, nothing ever remains the same. You're changing, whether you like it or not! Just by remaining static, you've made a change. You've stopped change from happening.

That's the big racecourse over there. You know, it all used to be open before, everyone could just walk in to watch the horses, but what happened? They fenced it in because people were throwing stones and fireworks at the horses, all kinds of things. How utterly low is that? That is a lack of education. Shocking. It seems worse now than it ever was. All this technology is breaking our connection with the reality around us.

(stopped in solid traffic again)

When I think of Australia, the gentleness people show towards the animals at the zoo... You're allowed within the same enclosures as the animals themselves; the kangaroos will take the food from your hand!

I think to grow up in that kind of care towards life is good. I like to watch our students play with the cats at school, especially that black and white one.

NF: What's your idea of progress?

SC: In many cases, progress is regress. People just want to build things instead of looking at the terrain and organizing it in harmony with the land. Progress can improve the lot of humans, while at the same time maintaining the environment, which is, of course, very much part of improving their lot. If you can't protect the environment, you can't improve humans.

If I go up there to the big bridge, will I get lost? Yes, let's have a little adventure, shall we?

NF: Which bridge is that?

SC: Oh, don't ask me.

You know, driving around like this, when I could be in school teaching math and science, is wonderful. (Driving fast and free over the bridge)

NF: What's the worst situation you've ever found yourself in?

SC: Oh dear, oh dear, oh dear... One I'll never forget was as a novice when I was supposed to call all the sisters early one morning, so I dutifully called up each one, or so I thought. Then they sent for me. "Do you realize you forgot to call Mother whatever-her-name-was, she missed Mass this morning!" A mortal sin. I was devastated. What have

I done? I knew I had called her, but she must have gone back to sleep again, and then all of them started complaining that they had never been called either, so my entire world seemed to have turned against me, and I felt like I was going to be hung at the gallows. I said sorry to them all, but I did feel terrible.

Now, maybe there's a way of going through the toll booth without paying, let's see. (Driving towards the concrete toll booth) 'Truck, trailer, minivan, carriage, jeep, 10 rupees.' (She pays the man in the toll booth.) Thank you. I'll go up here, turn around, and get onto the other side. (Traffic police stop us, look into the minivan, then wave us on.) Thank you, yes, thank you. That's what you get for being dressed like me. (Laughing) Otherwise, they'd have questioned you about filming with your camera in a place like this, oh yes. They know me, they would know a Sister, and very rarely do Sisters drive. Now, we're stuck on this expressway and I don't know how to get off. (Laughing a lot) I'm wondering where we are...

NF: Who's the most interesting person you've met?

SC: My God, your questions are impossible to answer! Jesus Christ, He's the most interesting one. Who else? Abdul Kalam, the former President of India. Who else? Bill Clinton. Who else? Mohammed Yunus in Bangladesh who began the Grameen Bank is a wonderful man.

Look, I've found a little opening in the road to turn around in.

It's very difficult to answer that!

NF: What did you talk to Clinton about?

SC: We talked about Ireland. All these people were coming up to him and pledging to take 10 million cubic tons of carbon out of the atmosphere and all that kind of carry-on. Then everyone received a certificate and had their photo taken with him. So when it was my turn, I said to him, "Why would you want a picture with me? I haven't done anything," and he replied, "What's fifty years in India, if it's not something?" Wasn't that nice? I met him a few times after that, and he always stopped to speak with me. He gave the most fantastic closing speech at the end of that UN thing; I wish I had recorded it.

There we go, turned around and on our way back home.

Who else have I talked to? Were you expecting me to say Mother Teresa?

NF: No. When I ask a question, I don't expect anything back.

SC: Oh right. Well, I thought Bill Clinton was extremely charming, and if his private life was so sleazy as it was made out to be, then why didn't his own wife divorce him? Why did she stand up for him? You know, public figures like him can be pilloried by unscrupulous ladies who have no shame.

Let's get ready to pay the toll again. Is there anything coming up behind us? No. Ok.

Bill Drayton is another one. The founder of the Ashoka Fellows, he had the idea that just as you have commercial entrepreneurs who start businesses and make lots of money, you also have social entrepreneurs, people who can take an idea and contribute to the improvement and development of society and justice and the human race. He selected people and paid their normal salary for three years, but when he came across me, I'd already developed much of Loreto Sealdah, so I wasn't able to get a grant from him. He instead made me a selector of other entrepreneurs as well as an Ashoka Fellow. I am a social entrepreneur. He asked me how much time I spent every day in creative thinking, and I'm the only person, he said, to have answered, "All my waking hours."

(She shouts at a big, blue local bus coming across right in front of us.) Hey, I'm going this way, this way, yes. (She gives a little head bow to the bus driver.) Thanks.

NF: Kolkata is full of people, isn't it?

SC: Look, he's going all over the place in front of me, and telling me to stick to my lane. (Laughing loudly) Yes, very warm people. (Paying the toll) Thank you. Okay, and we escaped the police on the other side. They check a lot if you're smuggling stuff in and out.

NF: What kinds of things?

SC: Drugs. It's not a problem, compared to other places. What you don't get here is people just getting killed, like in New York. If someone gets killed here, there's a reason for it.

Look at that great, big fat car banging its way along the road, I want to get past it... Isn't it a beautiful bridge? (Sound of police sirens behind us)

My God, look at this idiot standing in the middle of the road, what's he doing?

I love the symmetry of it all, the whole river, beautiful. (Miles of river can be seen together with the city of Kolkata.) Next question.

NF: Who's your best friend?

SC: Who's my best friend? I've many, you know. (Laughing)

NF: Do you have a confidant?

SC: I've many. (Laughing more) There's lots of people I talk to, and there's lots of people I wouldn't talk to.

NF: If you had a serious problem, would you go to anybody with it?

SC: Yes, I would. I have some friends among the police who I have a very close relationship with to talk things over. There is one priest in particular I am very close to, who I can talk anything out with, anything, and a few nuns also. But I'm closer to the police for talking out people's problems, and they could help me more with that sort of thing.

I'm taking you back a different route.

NF: So, have you ever had a problem that you couldn't work out?

SC: Some problems are to be worked out, some problems don't have solutions...

(12:01 pm. We've run out of film. We saw no accidents...)

INTERLUDE

ONE OF MOTHER TERESA'S FAVOURITE JOKES...

Archbishop Fulton Sheen arrived in Chicago where he was to give a talk, but he got lost, so he asked some neighborhood boys, "Boys, can you direct me to Town Hall?"

"What are you going to do there?" a little one asked him.

"I'm going to give a talk on how to find God," he explained.

"How can you talk about finding God," the little one said, "when you can't even find Town Hall?"

THE STUDENT COUNSELLOR (PART 2)

Loreto has given us so much, that strength of character, where we are not frightened to reach out to people, whatever situation they may be in. For me, that is what this school has done, it's a huge learning experience. I don't remember, to be honest, what I was taught academically in class because I'm not using it in my daily life, but we are in the midst of people here, real people, who are an integral part of our lives and we can't overlook them.

If someone needs our help, we jump in, help out and later we can think about the formalities and legalities.

If you think of the children right in front of you, then you can think of another five children outside of that, but first you have to think of one. You do one, and you'll have the urge to do another, and if you're happy to do it for one, then you're happy to do it for a thousand.

It's like practice; practice makes perfect. So, touching human lives is also a kind of practice. If you don't practise, you say, oh, it's not my job.

Throughout the day at school, there are so many people who come in, and although I don't always have to meet them, there are some times when you're meant to meet somebody, you're meant, I feel that. And if you talk about God and spirituality and all that, God plans these things.

I've met people who really need to be taken care of—maybe I've missed many also—I still need to meet more people who need us or I need them.

It's a win-win situation, it works both ways. It's not that we're only giving, they give us a lot, too. Even a person off the street, a very poor person, a very old person, can give you a lot.

What can she give you?

A lot of joy, a lot of peace, a lot of satisfaction. You can't do this for money, so what you can't get with money, you look for in people.

There are failures, but I can't let them get to me. I have to think, "Okay, it didn't work with this one, but it'll work with someone else."

In the past, we took in old people off the street and allowed them to stay with us for several months, but then we found they wanted to return to their lives in the stations.

It was a disaster.

I can't tell you, I was in tears about it—to see them back where we first found them was terrible—but it was their choice to return, and we had to respect that. We had to move on, because you have to give that person the freedom, and you also have to give yourself the freedom to move on.

There are other people looking for opportunities to take shelter or a bed, so I have to look for that.

It's important, otherwise life stops, and there is no development, no growth in yourself. If your ego gets hurt, you stop reaching out to people, and after that, you stop living.

The biggest joy is in giving, the biggest joy. It all goes back to what I learned here at school—the values—and also from my family, especially my father who had a lot to give. I still remember, I had a dress and went to show it to a girl who had no dress, and my father scolded me, "You have a dress, but you shouldn't have gone and shown it to her because she doesn't have one; it will make her feel bad!"

It was a great lesson: you don't show off what you have. And yet, even though we were middle class, as a teenager I only had one dress to go out in, nothing fancy, fifteen members in our family, my father was the only earning member, so we'd seen many ups and downs. Seen poverty and bad times. So even now, when we're doing well, it hasn't made us lavish, we don't waste things, rather we simply try to give opportunities to other people.

If I have five dresses and two of them I don't really wear, then I give both away to someone who can use them.

That's our way.

That's our life.

MESSAGE FROM THE LORETO ALUMNI

We believe that:
Education must be open to all—
irrespective of caste or creed,
religion or race, income, or even talent.

We believe that:
Education is the liberating influence
that has the potential to change social equations.

We believe that:
Our Rainbow programme is not just a step ahead—
it is a revolution.

We believe that:
Together we can change some tears into smiles of joy.

We believe that:
Imparting education to the Rainbows is not our responsibility—
it is our duty.

We believe that:
Two hours after school does not mean teaching—
it means that we care.

We believe that:
It is up to us to show the world that we can.

We believe that:
We have just created ripples in the water...
the wave is yet to come

We believe that:
We have it in ourselves to go for it—and you?

PART X

Thoughts on Retirement

Three Years Later: January 2014

Things I Find Difficult

Being Lost

Seya: One We Couldn't Reach

...And Others We've Saved

What Am I Doing Now?

The Acorn Story

THREE YEARS LATER: JANUARY 2014

Loreto Schools are all over the world. Wherever you go, you'll find the same kinds of values, the same way of proceeding.

When I was transferred to Loreto Day School in Sealdah in 1979, I had no baggage as it were, I had nothing to leave behind. I just moved from Loreto House and began to find out as much as I could about the new school.

But, when I retired in 2013, I was leaving behind a school which had outreached into so many other areas of Kolkata: the brickfields, Eastern Bypass, all those areas of terrible need and poverty, where I knew we were able to make a difference in the lives of those people, maybe not in fantastic ways, but enough. So, I had to leave that behind not knowing how it would go. That was my challenge, to be able to walk out and not go back. That hurt a lot.

That was difficult, very difficult.

Meeting that challenge was very different from the challenges I faced before because they were all positive challenges and were all outside of myself: sick children, poor people with no education. All of that was outside of myself, so I could deal with it, and I had the machinery to deal with it. But when I retired, I had to leave something that for thirty-four years I had built up and put a lot of effort into.

I returned to Ireland for seven months, which is the longest I've ever been out of India. At first, I wasn't sure how I felt about it all, but fortunately, when I walk away from something and I find myself in a completely different situation, I'm always fully in that new situation and don't think too much about what was before.

In my last few years at Loreto Sealdah—as I got older, and a bit more tired—I often thought how I'd love to just stretch out flat and sleep. When all those decisions had to be made, I'd sometimes think, can you keep them all away from me for a while, can you give me a little rest? It would be nice for things to be all over and be peaceful, to have nothing to do, to be able to read those books I'd given up, play mahjong on my computer.

Absolutely nothing to do sounded quite attractive.

And now, there I was, retired, with days and days of rest stretching out in front of me and nothing to do!

So when I was contacted by the Education Department of the Indian Government, and when they asked me to become a consultant...

Well, let me just say it wasn't too hard to come out of retirement!

THINGS I FIND DIFFICULT

To sit down and do nothing. That's difficult.

Sometimes it's difficult to pray in that very silent way when God doesn't seem to be anywhere around, you're just there in his presence.

I read a book the other day about a lady who can cure people, but she says it isn't her doing the curing, it's God. She prays over people who come to her, God's power goes through her, and the sick people get up and walk away cured, as they did in Jesus's time. I've developed a terribly bad back and bad legs, which make it hard to walk, and I try to say, "Thank you, Jesus," every time I'm walking, and the pain goes away, at least in one leg anyway.

In my life, I've always hesitated to ask for help for any of my aches and pains, because I don't believe I should. I ask for help for others but not for myself, but now having read that book, I think, why shouldn't I ask for myself? Maybe He would like to cure me, too. I'm going to find out, but the pain is much less when I ask.

It's very difficult to stand up for myself if someone is bullying me or saying nasty things or doing things they shouldn't. It's no problem for me to stand up for others and shout and be a bully myself, but when it happens to me, I find it very hard.

I find it very hard not to be on good relations with everybody around me. It upsets me very badly. If I've offended someone or done something hurtful, I can't rest until I go back and apologize and mend the fences that were broken. I need to have all my relationships in good order.

Anything else? Keeping my things tidy, but having said that, God is looking after me because if I really need to find something, it's there.

I would find it very hard to be cruel to a child or an animal. I couldn't bear it. I hate to see an animal suffering, it's extremely difficult for me. Some people say I'm too soft so I get taken advantage of, and yes, maybe some people do that, but I'm usually too cute to let that happen.

And, of course, retiring from Loreto Sealdah was very hard.

BEING LOST

Have I ever been lost inside of myself? Have I ever been lost? I don't think so. I've always been very aware of myself, aware of my reactions, things that happen to me. I'm very aware of my interactions with other people.

I wonder how people get lost?

They don't know what to do, or where to go. People often say, "Oh, it's easy for Sister Cyril, she's really lucky." It's funny, people outside of India think so highly of all the things I've done, but the ones inside India can't afford to think too highly of me because they might realize they should be doing the same thing. They shy away because they feel guilty.

Actually, I felt a little lost when I retired. I went through two or three very tough months, but now I'm busy on a day-to-day level.

I do look forward to what's going to happen next, but I think, how long to go before I die, how many more years do I have with this pain, how many more times can I say, thank you, Jesus, for removing the pain?

I'm not looking forward to dying, but at the same time I'm not frightened. I don't think, oh, it'll be great to die now. I'm quite happy as I am, and I know I'm doing something useful, and I'll continue until I lose my capacities either in my head or my legs.

I hope my head doesn't go first.

I have one small jealousy watching other people older than me running up and down the stairs, passing me with no trouble at all.

It's important for me to feel useful, but I'd like it not to be so important. I would like to think it's fine if I can just sit down and say I'm not useful anymore. It would be nice to sit on the shelf.

Within myself, I sometimes wish I could have a heart attack or an accident. People would say, "Oh, she's sick now, we won't bother her." But people do bother me because they think I'm still capable of helping them. Something would have to happen to me to stop doing it all. I need an excuse to do nothing.

I like the joke about the little boy whose constantly reprimanding mother called him in and said, "What are you doing, Johnny?" and he replied, "I'm doing nothing!" She gave him a clip on the ear and said, "Well, get out and do something, you lazy little bugger!"

SEYA: ONE WE COULDN'T REACH

She lived in a lean-to shanty next to the hospital across the road from the school. One night, when she was very young, she got up to go to the toilet; somebody grabbed her, raped her, and she bled a lot. She was put into a hospital and when she was eventually let out, I wanted to take her as a school boarder so she could be near me, but the hospital staff wanted to put her somewhere outside the city. Her mother brought her over to me, but her brother, three years older than Seya, kept repeating, "Stay home, stay home." Her mother had no choice because she loved him.

Seya grew up. She learned everything by heart, counted by heart, read. I knew she was clever, but nothing actually seemed to go into her brain. Her brother was very clever, too, but died of a tumour on his brain stem. She went to school but never learnt anything, she could just repeat things; we never seemed to be able to reach into her.

She always wanted attention. Any stranger she met she would immediately cling on to, and we did manage to help her grow out of that a little.

As she grew older, I realized she would need more professional help than we could give her, so we sent her to Sanlaap, an organization that deals with trafficked children, ones who had been sold off and then brought back by the police. They are very good, do a lot of counselling, and we often exchanged children with them.

They took Seya for six months but told us they couldn't do anything for her, because she didn't want to change. She wanted to stay the way she was. At the age of twenty, she came back to us, too old for school, so many things she didn't want to do. Her father had died, and her mother had gone back to live in her small village in rural Bihar.

I explained the situation to her mother and told Seya that if she returned to the village she could earn a living by teaching English, which by then she spoke very well. She settled down, but I always considered her one of my failures because I could never reach her.

Strangely, everybody loved her. She was quite a popular child at school, but we couldn't get her to change or to grow, and she remained as she was, an enigma.

Later, she fell in love with my nephew, wrote a long love letter—all in the third person—about all the things inside of her that she couldn't get to the outside...

...AND OTHERS WE'VE SAVED

Do you remember Jayna? The eleven-year-old who looked a bit like a fish and would take off all her clothes and run around screaming if she didn't get her way?

She visited me recently with another girl, full of life, gave me a big, big hug, and is doing very well in Class 9. She is now fourteen. I had to remind myself that this is the girl I put back in kindergarten only two years ago, so, within a very short time, she's progressed a lot.

The other girl who came with her, Nadi, slightly younger, was another problem child, having been abandoned on a train platform with her older sister when they were quite old. Their mother told them she'd be right back, then disappeared, but some kind soul found them and brought them both to us, where they have stayed ever since. The older sister, Tanaz, was a winsome little girl, and Nadi was deadly jealous of her, which made her all tied-up inside and a very poor student. But, to my joy, I now found her smiling away, telling me all about open-school, doing business studies, sociology, English, computers and home management. I'd personally chosen those subjects for her because the open-school students are the ones who can't cope with huge amounts of lessons and memorization, so all her subjects were practical.

And there was Jayna, large as life, proudly listening to her friend, on par with everyone else in Class 9.

She still looks long and lanky, very athletic, full of jazz, energy and joy, but she's always like that until someone crosses her for some reason. Any moment of injustice—she couldn't bear any form of injustice—was sufficient to change Jayna into a wild harridan of anger.

I remember one night hearing her scream, and finding her holding two plates of bread and butter, which she was supposed to take upstairs to the other girls, but got accosted by an older girl who took the bread off the plates. I caught the other girl red-handed, and since then, Jayna has always seen me as a source of justice.

Jayna isn't living at Loreto Sealdah now. I'm not sure if this is a temporary or permanent thing, but she has always been lucky with her sponsors. This has enabled one of her supporting groups to put aside her sponsorship money into a separate account for her to use when she goes to college.

And do you know what she told me she wants to become after she graduates?

A teacher.

WHAT AM I DOING NOW?

Right now, I'm working for the National Commission for the Protection of Children's Rights (NCPCR), which is responsible for seeing that all children get the entitlements regarding education under the Right to Education Act. This means they are supposed to get free schooling between the ages of six and fourteen, in addition to their uniforms, their meals, books, everything.

Yet, in most cases, they don't.

The second area of concern is the whole idea of "inclusive schooling." The government is taking many children who have never been to school before, and putting them into class according to their age, not their ability. A twelve-year-old with no schooling can't possibly keep up with an educated child the same age, and I'm sure it's not very pleasant for them. The government has been trying to prepare for what we call "accelerated learning" for these children, for which Loreto Sealdah has provided a lot of the materials.

I'm particularly concerned about inclusive schooling because up to now, many low-caste children have been child labourers, and higher-caste children who normally took advantage of the free government schooling are now objecting to being in the same class as these local children. In some places, but not everywhere, the teachers are also from the higher castes, and they tend to put the lower-caste children at the back of the classroom. So of course, the new kids aren't going to be able to follow as well, and these are the ones who are already slower due to never having been at school in the first place! It's a bit of a mess.

When I got back to India, my first job was to set up 15 Rainbow Homes similar to the one I had set up in Sealdah. I got to choose the NGOs for that project, and we're just about to embark on the training for that. The Education Department has given me three girls who'll go around and check up on everyone, and my job is simply to keep it all running and make sure things happen.

The biggest challenge is that the Rainbow Homes are only supposed to keep the children until they are fourteen years old, so I'll have to see what can be done; they can't just be thrown back out on the street at that age! There need to be provisions made that take them up to age 18, and that will be a real challenge, as I have to negotiate with the Indian Government to get things changed. I'll need to move around and find people who can work with me, stand up for me, fight for me.

But, it will get done.

They also asked me to improve the quality of education at the elementary level in West Bengal. So we're penetrating into 600 elementary schools to spread the concept of social justice and anti-discrimination. In each school, we're developing teams of nine children and three teachers who have been taught to do accelerated learning, to search and befriend children out on the street and bring them into school.

I am continuing my work but on a broader level and with more influence in those wider circles, but when you move into government, you realize there are seven million children in West Bengal schools alone.

Another fight I'll have on my hands is all the tribal children who are in the Catholic schools out in the remote areas, and none of them get a midday meal because those schools are not registered. Those kids are very poor, so I need to fight for them, too.

I think I'm going to be very, very busy...

That's my retirement. Basically, that's what is in front of me!

Better than doing nothing.

But whenever I feel a bit overwhelmed by it all, or old, or tired, I think back to my image of the acorn, and then I'm perfectly happy.

Would you like to hear about the acorn?

THE ACORN STORY

A while ago, I was participating in a course on transition, and we were given homework to find a symbol in nature which would speak to us about transition, epitomize it.

I forgot to do this work, so the next day, when everyone was putting their symbols down on the table in front of us, I realized I had nothing.

As I was sitting there, blank, wondering what I would do when my turn came, this acorn popped into my head, totally uninvited, but it was there, and I realized this was the symbol of my transition.

I see my acorn riding up on top of the oak tree with everything it could possibly need for its survival—just as I had done every day at Loreto School, everything at my disposal—but suddenly the wind comes and blows my acorn off the tree and down onto the path. And lying there on the path I realize I have two choices.

One is to continue lying on the path and shrivel up and die.

And the other is to get into the grass, bury myself, and break wide open and create a new oak.

As I explained this to everyone, I realized suddenly, surprisingly, that it no longer mattered what happened to me because it was in God's hands, and I could safely leave it in His hands for the future.

And that has given me a great sense of peace and joy.

So... that's it.

That's the end.

Student arriving at school

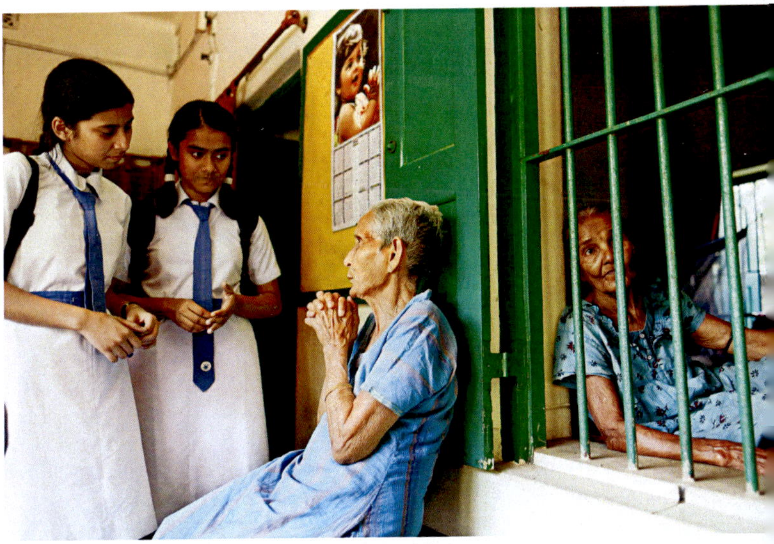

Outreach programme: lending a sympathetic ear

Outreach programme: a village classroom

Outreach programme: Loreto girls teaching village children

Playing at school

Dancing, anywhere, anytime

A Loreto teacher playing with Rainbow children

Morning rituals before class

Sister Cyril doing what she loves

A 6-year-old tending to a baby at Brickfields

Getting ready for a lesson at Brickfields

Administrative duties

The school van, a symbol of the generosity of others

Sister Cyril crossing the footbridge in front of her school

Morning announcements

Expanding young minds

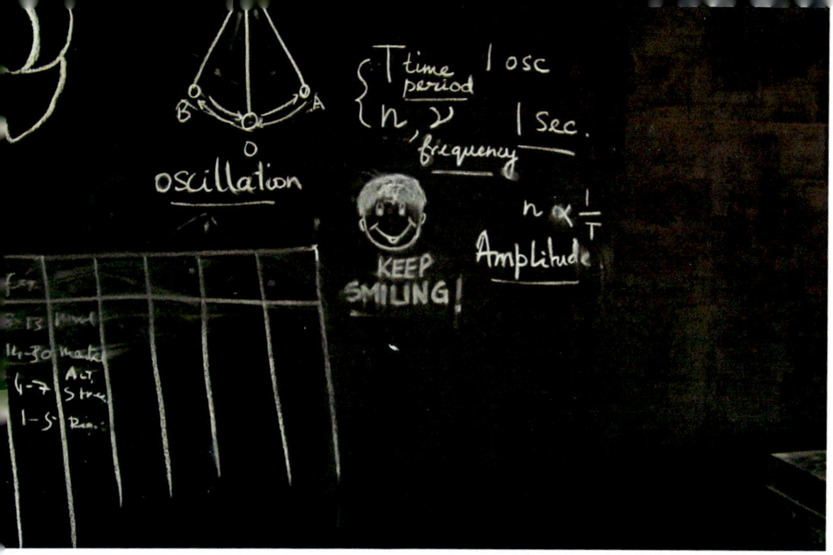

Learning with a smile

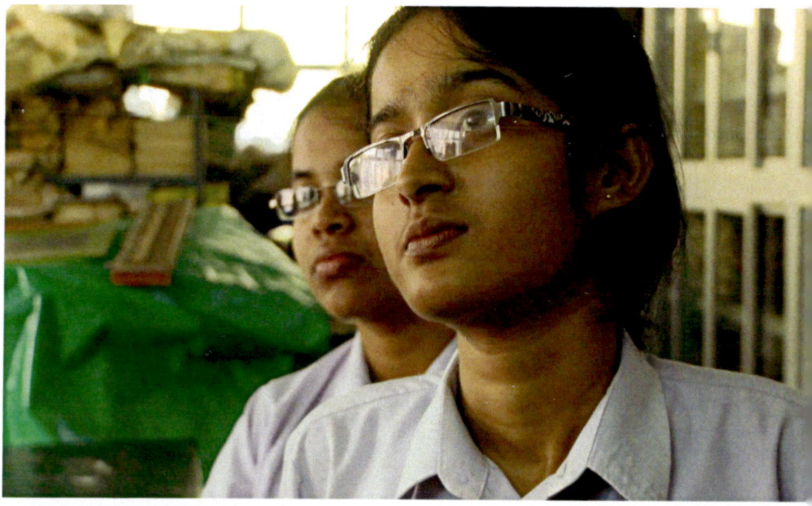

Taking their studies seriously

The wonderfully chaotic courtyard at Loreto

School bus arriving with students

A Rainbow child

Future leaders

APPENDIX

AWARDS

1) UNESCO International Award, the NOMA Award for spreading literacy and education amongst the poorest

2) Telegraph Award for Social Service—1997-2001, 2003, 2004, Hall of Fame 2005

3) Telegraph Award for Creative Excellence—2000

4) Telegraph Award for Best School—2002

5) Linda Finch, Great Lady Aviator, nominated Loreto Day School Sealdah as the beneficiary of the award presented to her by the Amelia Earhart Birthday Centennial Committee 1998

6) Better Kolkata Award for Outstanding Performance—2000

7) International Christian Stewardship Award, Toronto—2002

8) CINI—friend of CINI Award

9) Ladies Study Circle—'Woman of the Year'

10) Alexander Award for Excellence in Science—2007

11) Padma Shri for Social Work of a High Order—2007

12) National HRD Network 11th National Conference—2007

13) International Stewardship Award, Bishops of Toronto—2007

14) Honorary Doctorate in Education, Trinity College, Dublin—2010

15) Global Visionary Award, University of Monmouth, New jersey, USA—2011

16) Honorary Doctorate in Humane letters, University of Manitoba, Canada—2012

17) Honorary Doctorate in Humane Letters, Hope University, Liverpool—2012

18) Distinguished Service Award, President of Ireland—2013

Q&A FROM STUDENTS

1) What actually inspired you to come to India and do service for the poor?

I was constantly in touch with the Provincial of India, who became the Principal at Loreto Bray in Ireland. She was always telling us about India, and I remember seeing photographs of the Himalayas, and deep inside myself, I always felt called to India, although in fact, my mother was a great missionary for Africa. I was constantly exposed to Africa rather than India.

When I took my vows, the Mother General sent for me and asked where on the foreign missions I wanted to go. "I leave that up to you," I replied, and when she told me "India," it was a confirmation of what I felt inside.

2) What was the toughest thing about leaving Ireland to come here?

Leaving the beauty of the countryside behind, and my family, my parents, my brother and sister, my friends, some of whom I've continued to see after 60 years.

3) How long is your hair (we've never seen it!)? How many times a year is it cut? Do you like short hair or doesn't it grow?

My hair grows, definitely, like everyone else's. I normally cut it myself because it's usually tucked under my veil so it doesn't matter what shape it takes. I keep it short, but as a child in Ireland, I was known for my plaits. I had two very long ones.

4) From where do you draw your inspiration?

My ultimate inspiration is from Jesus and my relationship with God, and my secondary inspiration is drawn from the situations I see in front of me, because, at heart, I'm a problem solver.

5) What is the biggest regret of your life?

Never being able to speak an Indian language properly so that I could take part in an erudite meeting, a conversation. I'm always conscious of, even now, when working with the government, that everyone is trying to talk to me in English, because if I wasn't there, they'd all be speaking in Bengali. I used to try, every holiday, to study Bengali, but then I'd lapse back into English and I'd forget everything I learnt.

It hasn't cut me off from people, though, because I think our strongest communication is a smile.

6) What place do you find most peaceful?

The chapel, particularly, the one upstairs because the chairs are so comfortable. The shape fits me, and I don't get a sore back, and I can rest my arms. It makes a difference to me, and it makes things peaceful.

If I am in Ireland, then out in nature, sitting under the trees.

7) Have you ever been offered a bribe for school admission?

No, but I'm aware of someone else who took a bribe for a school I was working in. A father was desperate to get his niece into our school. The girl took the test and passed, far ahead of everyone else in the class. Afterwards, when asked, the father told me he'd paid someone in the Education Department 10,000 rupees (100 GBP) to secure a place for her. I told the man he was a big fool, he didn't need to do that, his child got in on her own good performance. I then rang up the person in question, told him what I had heard, and asked him to make sure he didn't do it again, and in future, I would not listen to any further petitions from him about admissions. He never contacted me again.

8) Do you really enjoy wearing the same habit that you always wear, or is it compulsory?

No, it's not compulsory, but this is my religious dress. I've seen foreigners like me trying to get into saris and I don't want to be mistaken for anybody's wife except Jesus's.

9) Do you always wear your habit wherever you go?

Yes, at all times. Not in bed, though. I once shared a hotel room in Mumbai with a Carmelite nun who slept on top of her bed fully clothed in her religious dress, headgear all perfect, with her hands together and her rosary wrapped around them, looking just like a corpse.

10) Do you miss your family?

Yes, I do. I miss the young ones growing up. I have eight nieces and nephews, but when I left, the eldest was only three. The next time I saw him, he was fifteen! They're all grown up now and have their own children. When I go home I see them, and we have great fun together. We're very much a family. When I'm there, I'm absolutely there, and when I'm not there we carry on with our lives.

11) Which was the most memorable day of your childhood?

The day of my first communion. And the day my cow, Dolly, died. And many sunny, sunny days, running through the fields in my bare feet, collecting primroses from the ditches and finding bluebells up in the woods.

12) Do you like chocolate?

Yes, I love chocolate, but not the black stuff. Chocolate with nuts is my favourite. Cadbury's. I don't eat much of it these days, because I don't want to put on any weight. I'm getting too sedentary, as it is.

13) Do you still hang your whistle beside your pocket?

No, I left my whistle in Loreto Sealdah.

14) If you had the chance to take up a cause at this point in your life, what would it be?

For the poor, to draw attention to the injustices they suffer.

15) What do you think of the molestation and harassment of girls taking place in India now?

It is detestable and dreadful. We can't put it into a book what I would do to the men who do these things. I wouldn't put them in prison. I would instead amputate one certain aspect of anatomy and leave them without it, then turn them loose so they can do nothing. Sticking them in prison doesn't help because when they leave, they repeat the offence.

But the really important point here is that not nearly enough is being done to educate boys in matters of sex. They are not properly educated in how to treat women and not properly educated about their own sex. Not enough understand at all, and unfortunately, girls are much more affected by the outcome than they are.

16) Have you ever climbed a tree eating a banana?

No, but I've climbed a tree eating an apple. You can't climb trees in Ireland eating bananas, and I certainly wouldn't do it in India.

17) Have you ever used someone else's toothbrush by mistake?

No, not even on purpose.

18) Have you ever sat on a chair that was too small for you?

No.

19) Have you ever tried to laugh without your eyes closed?

I actually do a whole workshop on different kinds of laughter. It's one of my party pieces. I've done a lot of research on laughter. Some people laugh on the breath coming in, some laugh on the breath going out, some laugh up and down the scale, some people slap themselves, others laugh just with their faces, some with their whole bodies.

Me? I just laugh!

20) In what way did God inspire you?

He inspired me to become a Loreto Sister on November 3, 1949, sometime that morning between 10:00 am and noon. I know this because I was sitting in a chapel at a retreat and the Father was talking to us, and among many other things, he said, "Go for the teaching of all nations," and like that, I knew inside of myself that's what God wanted me to do for the rest of my life. So, I sat there in the wonder of it all until 12:30, then the bell rang for lunch and I raced down the stairs, changed my shoes, jumped on my bike and pedalled home as fast as I could, burst in on my mother and shouted, "I'm going to be a nun!" She was cooking lunch at the time and said, "Oh, that's okay when you're old enough." I was thirteen at the time.

Four years earlier, my elder sister had written away to America after she'd seen an advertisement for nuns, but when they came around to our house to collect her, my mother stalled them with tea and biscuits because my sister had disappeared, having changed her mind about the whole thing. So, when I came along, she took it all very coolly.

I left home at seventeen, and here I am!

21) Did any incident ever make you feel like leaving India?

No. It's an interesting question. If people had spat at me and told me to get out of the country, I don't know, but I've never had anything in India but happiness and joy and people wanting me, rather than the opposite.

When I finished up at Loreto Sealdah in 2012, there were several Leadership Training Student (LTS) boys who had been with me for a long time, and who offered to let me stay in their homes where they could look after me.

22) Have you ever been hurt by someone?

Oh yes, of course, many times, but I'm not going to say how. When you have a fight with someone, "Let not the sun go down on your anger." I would always go back to that person and say sorry, even if I was not the one who did the offence, because I can't bear having a broken relationship in my life. If I was not able to forgive, I would not be able to pray.

23) Do you miss your 'Rainbows'?

Now, I know they're all waiting for me to say, "Yes, yes, of course I do," but the thing is this: I've got new Rainbows, another 1500 Rainbows around Kolkata. I'm always thrilled when my old Rainbows come and see me, but you can't live your life missing people.

24) Have you ever fallen in love with a man?

Jesus is the only man I've ever been in love with. I like men, I enjoy their company, I have many male friends, but I've never been in love with any of them.

25) Is the world changing, or are you changing the world?

The world is changing, not because of me. Yes, I make my own small contribution, but there are thousands of others out there making their contributions. Everyone is trying—actually is everyone really trying?

I wrote an education paper: "The Formation of Children to Take Their Place in Society and Contribute Positively to its Improvement." So, in that case, I've made another contribution to society, and I can see where some of the changes have come about, particularly in education and caring for the poor.

To some extent, the world changes by itself, but I think man's contribution is large, very large. I think man begins a huge number of chain reactions by the various positive and negative actions he does, and these bring about change to the world. When I think about Global Warming, man is largely responsible, and that means all of us.

26) Do you dance in your free time?

No, definitely not, at least not now since I hurt my back, but I did other things like swimming, running, playing tennis. Some of the Loreto girls remember me playing basketball with them, and winning. (Winning I remember as being very important!)

27) What was your very first thought when you arrived in India?

I wouldn't like to say it in public, I tell you. I remember, in 1956, very early one morning looking out over the side of the ship at the Mumbai docks and watching people dropping coins down towards all the little boats full of Indian children that surrounded us and watching them dive into the water for the money.

I remember riding a train and hanging out of the window the whole time and being completely covered in coal dust by the time we arrived in Kolkata, and being utterly intrigued watching the men ploughing the fields, with every inch of their bodies also completely covered.

28) Do you ever think you'll become a saint?

No. N-O. No! Categorically no!

29) Did society ever become an obstacle in your way?

Yes, constantly, because when you're pioneering something and pushing things ahead, pushing the boundaries and the barriers, you're going to get a lot of people who would prefer to keep the status quo. What I'm trying to do is make a paradigm shift from our big schools, where everybody pays fees with a few poor children attending, to a situation where the poor are on an equal footing and are 50 percent of the student intake. This kind of thinking does not meet with the approval of some people around me, including some Loreto Sisters. It's not that I was directly opposed, it's much more that I was ignored. I was ignored for a long time...

30) What incident gave you the strength to carry on with your work for the rest of your life?

There are constant incidents. I can't say there is any one, it's constant, and you need it every day. One incident is not sufficient to give you the strength to carry on for the rest of your life. It's an ongoing step-by-step process.

31) Do you always get the support you expect from other people?

Mostly yes, but sometimes no. If you look at it over the span of my entire life, the ones who wouldn't support me would be few and far between. I've rarely had anyone stand in front of me and say they wouldn't support me. People usually do help, and with regard to my work with the West Bengal government, all the Loreto schools have donated teachers to come and help out.

32) How do you feel having given so much of yourself to the Indian people?

After spending almost the whole of my life here, I know that I've been much loved by many Indians, and I've become very much a part of them. They've told me repeatedly I'm not a foreigner but an Indian like them.

It's funny, when I was in Mauritius giving a course, they opened it with a hymn, one of those dreadful, third-person songs, "He is my everything, He is my all." Then when we came to the next session, I asked one of the Hindus if they could sing one of their Hindu "paja," all about the goodness of God, which we all sang together, and I felt so at home listening to it, so relaxed and at peace. The Christian song really jarred me, and I realized how much Indian spirituality and culture I had imbibed without even realizing it. There is something so attractive about this country. So many people I know return to it again and again.

33) How many pairs of boots do you have?

One. I wear them all the time.

FINAL WORDS FROM ALUMNI AND TEACHERS

– You changed the lives of millions—transforming them into socially aware responsible individuals, totally altering their way of thinking, empowered with the weapon of education.

– You caught my dreams and taught me to be confident to turn them into reality, to stand up and readily take responsibility and be accountable for my actions, to support what is right, to voice my views against social evils, to question conventions, to surprise people with a readiness to work.

– We've all come across people who are great at criticizing society, but when it actually comes to extending help to make a difference... she is active, real, energizing, showing us that we mortals are capable of extraordinary work.

– She helped recognize the leader in me and made it possible for me to believe what I was capable of.

– She gave many teenage girls the fearlessness to walk down crowded Kolkata roads.

– The epitome of power, freedom, encouragement, devotion, resolution, she is our own mother when we need someone to guide us, she is a father who infuses qualities of steadfastness and discipline, she is a teacher when we need skills to win in life, she is an angel to the homeless, and she is our reason for being where we are today.

- I am a strong and driven individual—today, what I am is because of you.

- I belonged to a very affluent Bengali family. Being the youngest and most pampered, I was very finicky about food, threw away most of it, and as a result was often sick and missed a lot of school. Sister advised my parents to put those foods which I particularly disliked in my lunch box. Then she called me into her office and in a very gentle way explained that there were children just outside the school gates who didn't have enough to survive on, and that I should be thankful to my parents and God for everything I had. I was too young to understand it all, but from that day I never wasted anything again. I ate whatever I could eat and gave away the rest to the street children. That day is when I learned about the disparity in our society: A lesson learned for a lifetime.

- You inspired me to think beyond myself, to compete with myself and not others.

- If I make a difference by the way I think and feel and act it is because you touched me and I responded.

- I cannot tell you how valuable you are to the world.

- She showed me that reality is like cultivating a garden, and that those who would have nothing to do with thorns must never attempt to gather thorns.

- May the clock go on ticking and allow her to help others.

- The master maestro.

- A helping hand for any critical situation.

- Thank you for the opportunity to stand on my own two feet.

- You touch the real people of this world—a world that sadly believes in competition and consumerism, leaving these people far behind.

– Ordinary people like me have to be stimulated to make extraordinary efforts. She makes winners out of ordinary people.

– I never knew where to turn to, everything was dark in my life, I was afraid of my future, everything seemed finished, then I met you, and you immediately invited me to Kolkata. There was no turning back.

– You say, "The only way to develop India is by imparting quality education to all. Deprived children don't have any home support. We are the only hope for them. We are accountable only to them."

– I remember when you asked my dad what he planned for me. Like most fathers, he said an arranged marriage. He never told me your exact words, but you did try to convince him that along with marriage, a career was important, too. Little did he realize that his shy, introverted daughter could now plan her own future!

– Some people come into our lives and quickly go. Some stay a while, leave footprints in our hearts, and we are never, ever the same.

ONE LAST JOKE...

Did you hear of the old Irish woman whose son was away in the army? He wrote to tell her how hot it was where he was stationed: "40 degrees in the shade!"

"Dear son," she wrote back, "for God's sake keep out of the shade!"